Card Games

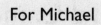
For Michael

Card Games

Sue Nicholson

p

This is a Parragon Book
First Published in 2002

Parragon
Queen Street House
4 Queen Street
Bath BA1 1HE, UK

Produced by Magpie Books, an imprint of
Constable & Robinson Ltd, London

ISBN 0–75257–786–7

A copy of the British Library Cataloguing-in-Publication Data
is available from the British Library

Printed and bound in the EU

ACKNOWLEDGEMENTS
Illustrations courtesy of Pascal Thivillon
Cover design by Slatter-Anderson

Contents

Children's Card Games I   **313**
(for younger children)

Introduction

This book contains the rules of over one hundred different card games, from simple solitaire to games of skill, such as Bridge, Poker and Whist.

The games have been arranged alphabetically in families, so if you're looking for a particular game check out the index in case it has been grouped with other, similar games.

You'll also find a list of good games for two, three and four or more players at the back of the book – just in case you have a certain number of people willing to play cards and can't agree on the best game to play!

Difficulty ratings
Most of the games in the book do not take much time to learn or to play once you are familiar with the rules. However, difficulty ratings have been given throughout. These are intended simply as a rough guide, mainly because some people are able to pick up the rules of play much more quickly than others and also because, even though the rules of a game may be grasped easily, to play it well often requires a great deal of practice and skill. The difficulty rating ranges from 1 to 3, with 1 being the easiest and 3 being the most difficult.

Rules and regulations
Even in a book of this length, it is impossible to include every type of card game or every variation of a particular game – there are over one hundred types of Patience alone and many versions of games such as Hearts and Poker. Similarly, rules often change with time or may vary from region to region. The rules given for each game

therefore are, on the whole, the most common. There's no harm in changing the rules slightly in informal games, though, as long as everyone is clear on the rules at the outset.

Most rules and regulations simply make sure that games go smoothly and there are no serious disputes. In formal games, there are obviously more rules regarding cutting the cards, seating and dealing. These rules have been given, where they apply, for each game. Although rules are clearly given, we have not included much information on strategy. Whole books have been devoted to how to play single games such as Bridge and Poker, so it would obviously be impossible to give them the deserved amount of space here. The best way to learn a game is to play it, especially with someone who has played it before. And in more formal games such as Bridge or Partnership Whist, there's usually no shortage of experienced players who are willing to offer advice!

Money matters

Several card games – including some children's games – are traditionally gambling games. All these games can be played with beans, matchsticks or any other suitable counters as the stake. Brag and Poker are often played with chips representing money or cash itself. If playing for money stakes, the cardinal rule is obvious and simple – never gamble more than you are able, and prepared, to lose!

In order to make it as quick and easy as possible to pick up the rules of forgotten or unfamiliar games, most card terms have been explained in the instructions so you don't need to keep referring to a glossary. A few terms that you will need to be familiar with, however, are explained overleaf.

Card Terms

ante A stake made before a game begins.

bid An offer to win a given number of tricks, often in exchange for choosing the game or trump suit.

carte blanche A hand without any court cards.

court card Kings, Queens and Jacks.

cut Either 1) To lift up the top part of a pack of cards to reveal the underneath card, often done to determine which player deals first, or 2) to lift up the top part of a pack of cards and place it under the rest of the cards to make sure that no player knows what the bottom card is.

declare To make a bid for or announce the type of game or trump suit for the game, or to show and score on held cards.

deuce A two in any suit.

discard To play an unwanted card in a trick.

draw To take or be dealt a card from the pile of stock or wastepile.

foundation A row of cards that are built on in games of Patience.

go out To play the last card in a hand.

hand The cards dealt to each player in a round or game.

honours A card or cards that award bonus points to the player who wins them in a trick, or simply holds them at the start of the play.

lead To play the first card of a trick.

meld A combination of cards that can be scored on (see Rummy and Bezique).

overtrick A trick that is over or in excess of the number of tricks needed to win a game.

pot or pool A number of counters (or money) staked by the players in a game which goes (in whole or in part) to the winner or winners.

prial Three cards of the same rank. (sometimes called a pair-royal).

rank The denomination of a card (rather than its suit), such as a King, ten or five.

revoke To not play a card of the same suit as the lead card in a trick, even when able to do so. (This usually incurs a penalty.)

rubber A match comprising several games (usually three).

sequence A run of three or more cards, such as King-Queen-Jack or two-three-four.

slam A bid to win every trick or winning every trick in a game.

stock Cards left over after the deal which may be drawn or dealt out during the game.

suit Hearts, diamonds, clubs and spades, each containing 13 cards.

trey A three in any suit.

trick A set made up of one card from each player in the game, which is won by the highest lead card or the highest trump card if a trump card is played.

trump A card of a chosen suit that will beat a card of any other suit when played in a trick.

undertrick A trick that is under or less than the number of tricks needed to win a game.

wastepile A pile of discarded cards, which is usually face up.

widow A number of cards dealt face down at the beginning of a game. In some games, one or more players may pick it up or exchange some of their cards for it.

wild card A card that is used to represent another card. Wild cards are usually the Joker or a chosen number card, such as the twos.

Belote

Belote is the national card game of France in which the aim is to reach an agreed number of points by winning tricks and declaring melds (groups of cards of the same rank or a sequence). It is a good game for two or three players, or for four players playing in partnerships.

Belote

Difficulty rating
2

Number of players
2–4

Cards
32, with all cards below seven (except the Aces) removed from a
52-card pack.

To win
Be the first player to reach a certain number of points (for example,
1000) over several deals.

To deal
Cut the cards to decide who is going to deal first and take it in turns
to deal. If there are three or more players, then the deal (and the first
turn to play) passes to the right.

The dealer deals six cards to each player in two sets of three and
turns the next card face up for trumps.

To score
Each card has a points value and points are awarded by adding up the
points value of cards in each won trick and by declaring melds – four
cards of the same rank, or a sequence of cards of the same suit (see
overleaf).

The player who chooses trumps is expected to score more points
than the other player, or players. If the player does not do so, then he
or she has to pay a penalty.

Trump suit
Ace – 11 points
Jack – 20 points
Nine – 14 points
Ten – 10 points
King – 4 points
Queen – 3 points

Other suits
Ace – 11 points
King – 4 points
Ten – 10 points
Queen – 3 points
Jack – 2 points

Melds
Four Jacks – 200 points
Four Nines – 150 points
Four Aces – 100 points
Four Tens – 100 points
Four Kings – 100 points
Four Queens – 100 points

Any sequence of cards of the same suit, from sevens to Aces:
Five or more cards – 100 points
Four cards – 50 points
Three cards – 20 points

 200 points

 150 points

100 points

 Sample sequence of five cards (lowest)

 Sample sequence of five cards (highest, if tied)

Scoring in Belote

To play

The non-dealer (or the player to the immediate right of the dealer if more than two players are in the game) can accept the turned-up trump card as the trump suit or may pass and the dealer, or the next player, can then choose to accept the trump suit or pass. If the dealer passes, then the first player can propose another suit. If he or she does not, then the dealer (or the next player if three are playing) can name the suit. If no suit is named the game does not continue and the cards are re-dealt.

Once the trump suit has been selected, the dealer deals three extra cards to each player and turns the bottom card of the pile of stock face up. (This is for information only as the trump suit has already been selected.)

Either player holding a seven of any suit can exchange it for the turned-up trump card. This exchange must be made before either (or any) player declares any melds.

Before playing the first trick, the dealer tells the other player or players what his or her highest meld is, based on its points value (four Jacks being the highest). The player need not tell the other player or players exactly which cards he or she holds. Only as much information need be given as is necessary to identify who holds the highest meld.

In determining which sequence is higher:

• A longer sequence (five cards or more) beats a shorter sequence.

• If two sequences are equal, then a trump sequence beats a sequence of cards in any other suit.

- If two sequences are still equal, then the dealer wins.

If the other player, or players, cannot better the dealer's declared meld, then he or she says "good" and the dealer scores points based on that meld and any other melds that he or she holds and declares.

If the other player, or players, can better the dealer's declared meld, then he or she tells the other(s) what his or her highest meld is and scores points accordingly. He or she also scores points for any other melds that he or she holds and is willing to declare.

Tricks are won by playing a higher card of the same suit as the lead card, or by playing a trump card. If more than one trump card is played, then the highest trump wins the trick.

In addition, points are scored as follows:

- The winner of the final trick scores an additional 10 points ("dix de der").

- If there are two players, the winner of the final trick scores a further 100 points ("capot") if he or she has won all nine tricks. If there are three players and one player does not win a single trick, the other two players each score 50 points for "capot". If there are three players and two players do not win a single trick between them, the third player scores the full 100 points.

- The holder of both the King and Queen of trumps scores 20 points when playing either of them in a trick and saying "Belote". If he or she does *not* say "Rebelote" on playing the second of the two cards, the 20 points awarded for playing the first card are taken away again.

At the end of the hand, the players announce their total points for melds and played cards. The score of the player who did not choose trumps stands. The score of the player who did choose trumps stands if he or she took more than declared. If he or she took less, then the score is added to that of the other player. If it is the same, then the score is held over and is awarded to the winner of the next hand.

Bezique

Bezique originated in France around 350 years ago. One of its variations, called Pinochle, is popular in the United States. Bezique is played with two or more piquet decks — that is, packs of cards in which all cards below seven (except the Aces) are removed. Pinochle is similar to Bezique except that it is played without the sevens and eights.

Bezique

Difficulty rating
2

Number of players
2

Cards
Two packs, with all cards below seven (except the Aces) removed from each pack, making a total of 64 cards (or a double Piquet deck). Aces rank high, followed by tens, Kings, Queens and Jacks down to sevens.

High   Low

Ranking of cards in Bezique

To win
Be the first player to reach an agreed number of points (usually 1000 or 2000) over several deals by scoring points in "brisques" (won tricks containing an Ace or a ten) and declared melds (cards of the same rank or sequences of cards).

To deal

Cut the cards to decide which player deals first. The dealer then deals out eight cards in packets of three, then two, then three, starting with his or her opponent.

The dealer turns up the next card to show trumps and places it face up under the pile of stock so that part of the card can be seen. If this card is a seven, then the dealer immediately scores 10 points.

To score

Scores are usually kept on paper. However, special bezique markers or cribbage boards are sometimes used instead.

500 points – double bezique (two Queens of spades and two Jacks of diamonds)

250 points – sequence of Ace, ten, King, Queen and Jack of trumps

100 points – any four Aces

80 points – any four Kings

60 points – any four Queens

40 points – any four Jacks

40 points – Bezique (one Queen of spades and one Jack of diamonds)

40 points – royal marriage (King and Queen of trumps)

20 points – common marriage (King and Queen of any other suit)

10 points – for exchanging the turned-up trump card for the seven of trumps (the player holding the other seven of trumps gets 10 points when it is played in a trick)

10 points – for winning the last trick of the game

10 points – for every brisque (every won trick containing an Ace or a ten)

Penalties

10 points awarded to the other player if a player draws a card out of turn.

100 points awarded to the other player if a player holds more than eight cards at a time.

10 points deducted from a player's score and awarded to his or her opponent if the player plays to a trick before drawing a fresh card from the stock.

To play (first stage of the game)

Each player looks at his or her hand and works out an opening meld.

The non-dealer leads with the first card of the opening trick. The dealer then plays any one of his or her cards to complete the trick. The highest leading card wins the trick unless a trump card is played. If two trump cards are played, then the highest trump wins the trick. If both players play a card of the same rank and suit, the player leading the trick wins it.

At this stage in the game, players do not need to follow suit to complete a trick, so they do not need to play a trump card even if the lead card is a trump.

The winner of each trick can declare a meld, laying the cards in the meld face up on the table so that points can be scored on it. More than one meld can be declared after winning a trick, but only one meld can be scored at a time.

The cards just played in a trick are discarded and each player picks up a fresh card from the pile of stock. The cards placed on the table in a declared meld must remain there, face-up, until they are played in tricks or used to form new scoring combinations.

Cards placed on the table may be re-used in melds several times as long as the melds are different. For example, if the Queen of spades is used in a marriage to a King, the card can be used to score points in a single bezique (Queen of spades and Jack of diamonds) or four Queens but cannot be used to score points in a marriage to another King.

If a player scores points for a sequence of trump cards, he or she can not score points later for a single marriage contained in the sequence. However, it is possible to declare and score points on the marriage first then include the marriage in a sequence later, after winning another trick.

A player can declare double bezique either by placing all four cards in the meld on the table at once or by adding a single bezique to another single bezique already declared. If the player scores for two single beziques, however, he or she may not also score for the double bezique.

The player winning a trick and declaring a meld plays the lead card of the next trick. The game continues in this way until all the stock is used up. The players then move onto the second, and final, stage of the game.

During a game, it is important to remember which cards have already been played in tricks and declared by the other player because these are unavailable to form new scoring combinations. Each player must judge which cards to collect to form possible melds and which to discard in tricks. It is a good idea to win tricks with tens whenever possible because tens do not have any scoring value in a meld (except the ten of the trump suit, which scores in a sequence) but score ten points each when won in a trick.

One of the main tactics in the game is to win tricks only if you have a high-scoring meld to declare or if the trick contains a brisque and will score you ten points.

In hand (player 1)

Declared meld on table

Stock and turned-up trump card

In hand (player 2)

Declared meld on table

A game of Bezique in progress. The first player, having won the previous trick has declared a scoring combination of a quartet of Aces (worth 100 points) and will play the lead card of the next trick. The second player has previously scored Bezique (worth 40 points). He or she will discard the non-scoring eight and nine in subsequent tricks and hope to draw the second Queen of spades to score for double Bezique (500 points) or another King to score 80 points.

To play (second stage of the game)

Each player takes his or her cards from the table for the last eight tricks of the game. The winner of the previous trick leads with the next card. At this stage in the game, no melds can be declared after a trick has been won and players must follow suit with the lead card. A player can only play a trump card if he or she cannot play a card of the same suit as the lead card.

The winner of the final trick scores an extra 10 points.

At the end of the game, each player counts the number of tricks containing either an Ace or a ten (called brisques) and scores 10 points for each.

If neither player has reached the target of 1000 or 2000 points, then the cards are redealt.

Bezique for three players

Bezique can be played with three players by using three piquet decks of cards (that is, 96 cards in total). In this case, the first player to score a target of 1500 points is the winner.

Partnership Bezique

Bezique can be played with four players in partnerships, with partners sitting opposite each other. Partnership Bezique is played with six piquet decks of cards (that is, six decks of standard cards each with the sixes, fives, fours, threes and twos removed, making a total of 192 cards).

After winning a trick, a player may declare his or her own meld or get his or her partner to declare a meld. A player can use any cards in a partner's declared meld to make further scoring combinations.

Scoring is similar to Six-deck Bezique (see page 25) with the following differences:

40,500 points – sextuple Bezique
13,500 points – quintuple Bezique
1000 points – any four Aces
900 points – any four tens
800 points – any four Kings
600 points – any four Queens
400 points – any four Jacks
500 points – double carte blanche (when both partners are dealt hands which contain no court cards (that is, no Jacks, Queens or Kings)

Four-deck Bezique (Japanese Bezique)

Number of players
2

Cards
Four piquet decks, or four standard 52-card packs with all cards below seven (except Aces) removed, making a total of 128 cards.

To win
Be the first player to reach an agreed number of points (usually 1000 or 2000).

To deal
Each player is dealt nine cards, either singly, or in packets of three.

To choose trumps

The next card is not turned up for trumps and the trump sevens have no points value. Instead, trumps are chosen according to the first sequence of cards or the first marriage declared in a meld and that trump suit stays the same throughout the whole game.

To change "Bezique"

Players can change the definition of Bezique at the beginning of the game so that Bezique is the Queen of the trump suit together with a Jack of the opposite colour (for example, a Queen of hearts with a Jack of clubs, or a Queen of spades with a Jack of diamonds.) If players decide to play with this rule, then the trump suit for the whole game can be decided by the suit of the Queen played in the first Bezique (if the Bezique is declared before a marriage).

To score

Unlike two-pack Bezique, points are not scored for brisques (for each ten or Ace in a won trick) but are awarded for sequences in other suits apart from trumps. Players are also awarded points if they are dealt a hand containing no court cards (a "carte blanche").

Beziques

4500 points – Quadruple Bezique (four Queens of spades and Jacks of diamonds unless Bezique is redefined – see page 16)
1500 points – Treble Bezique
500 points – Double Bezique
40 points – Single Bezique

Quartets

100 points – any four Aces
80 points – any four Kings
60 points – any four Queens
40 points – any four Jacks

Sequences and marriages

250 points – trump sequence (Ace, ten, King, Queen, Jack)
150 points – non-trump sequence (Ace, ten, King, Queen, Jack)
40 points – royal marriage (King and Queen of trumps)
20 points – common marriage (King and Queen of any other suit)

50 points – for carte blanche
50 points – for winning the last trick of the game
500 points – for winning the game
500 points – for "crossing the rubicon" (a bonus scored by the winner if the loser does not reach the "rubicon", or target score for the game).

Rubicon, or target score for the game: 1000 points

To play

The game is played in the same way as standard Bezique with variations in dealing and choosing trumps as explained above.

Sequences of cards in plain suits (suits other than trumps) can be declared as well as trump sequences. Cards on the table in a declared meld can be re-formed into the same scoring combinations. For example, if a player declares a meld of four Aces then plays one of the Aces in a trick, he or she can re-form the remaining three Aces into a further meld of four Aces and score on the combination again.

If a player declares carte blanche, he or she must show all the cards in the hand to score the 50 points. If the player draws another non-court card from the stock after the next trick has been played, then he or she can show it and declare another carte blanche and score a further 50 points. The player can continue to score in this way until he or she draws a court card from the stock.

To win

At the end of a hand, each player's score is rounded down to the nearest 100 points. The player scoring the highest number of points wins the game. The winner also scores the difference in points between his or her score and that of the other player and a bonus number of points if the loser fails to cross the rubicon, or reach the target number of points specified for the rubicon in the game.

Six-deck Bezique (Chinese Bezique)

Number of players

2

Cards

Six piquet decks, or six standard 52-card packs with all cards below seven (except Aces) removed, making a total of 192 cards.

To win

Be the first player to reach an agreed number of points over several deals.

To deal

Each player is dealt 12 cards, either singly, or in packets of three. The next card is not turned up for trumps. Instead, trumps are chosen according to the first sequence of cards or the first marriage declared in a meld.

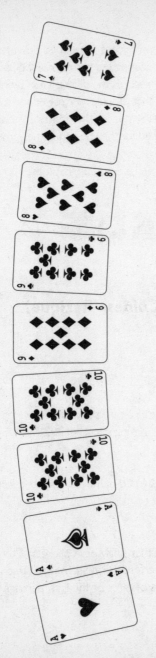

Carte blanche hand in four-deck Bezique (50 points)

To score

As with four-pack Bezique, points are not scored for brisques but are awarded for non-trump sequences. Points are also awarded for declaring "carte blanche". Additional points are scored for melding quartets of trump Aces, tens, Kings, Queens and Jacks.

Beziques

4500 points – Quadruple Bezique (four Queens of spades and Jacks of diamonds unless Bezique is redefined – see page 16)
1500 points – Treble Bezique
500 points – Double Bezique
40 points – Single Bezique

Quartets

1000 points – four trump Aces
900 points – four trump tens
800 points – four trump Kings
600 points – four trump Queens
400 points – four trump Jacks
100 points – any four Aces
80 points – any four Kings
60 points – any four Queens
40 points – any four Jacks

Sequences and marriages

250 points – trump sequence (Ace, ten, King, Queen, Jack)
150 points – non-trump sequence (Ace, ten, King, Queen, Jack)
40 points – royal marriage (King and Queen of trumps)
20 points – common marriage (King and Queen of any other suit)

250 points – for carte blanche
250 points – for winning the last trick of the game
1000 points – for winning the game

Loser's total number of points – for "crossing the rubicon" (a bonus scored by the winner if the loser does not reach the "rubicon", or target score for the game).

Rubicon, or target score for the game: 3000 points

To play
Play is the same as for four-deck Bezique except that trump quartets can be declared as well as non-trump quartets.

Eight-deck Bezique (Rubicon Bezique)

Number of players
2

Cards
Eight piquet decks, or eight standard 52-card packs with all cards below seven (except Aces) removed, making a total of 256 cards.

To win
Be the first player to reach an agreed number of points over several deals.

To deal
Each player is dealt 15 cards, either singly or in five packets of three. As with six-deck bezique, trumps are chosen according to the first sequence of cards or the first marriage declared in a meld.

To score

As with four and six-pack Bezique, points are not scored for brisques but are awarded for non-trump sequences. No points are scored for declaring carte blanche but additional points are scored for declaring trump quintets (five cards of the same rank and suit).

Beziques

9000 – Quintuple Bezique (five Queens of spades and Jacks of diamonds unless Bezique is redefined – see note on page 16).
4500 points – Quadruple Bezique (four Queens of spades and Jacks of diamonds unless Bezique is redefined).
1500 points – Treble Bezique
500 points – Double Bezique
40 points – Single Bezique

Quartets

1000 points – four trump Aces
900 points – four trump tens
800 points – four trump Kings
600 points – four trump Queens
400 points – four trump Jacks
100 points – any four Aces
80 points – any four Kings
60 points – any four Queens
40 points – any four Jacks

Quintets

2000 points – five trump Aces
1800 points – five trump tens
1600 points – five trump Kings
1200 points – five trump Queens
800 points – five trump Jacks

Sequences and marriages
250 points – trump sequence (Ace, ten, King, Queen, Jack)
150 points – non-trump sequence (Ace, ten, King, Queen, Jack)
40 points – royal marriage (King and Queen of trumps)
20 points – common marriage (King and Queen of any other suit)

250 points – for winning the last trick of the game
1000 points – for winning the game
Loser's total number of points – for "crossing the rubicon"

Rubicon, or target score for the game: 5000 points

To play
Play is the same as for four- and six-deck Bezique except that trump quintets can also be declared and no points are awarded for declaring "carte blanche".

Pinochle

Difficulty rating
2

Number of players
2

Cards
Two packs, with all cards below nine (except the Aces) removed from each pack, making a total of 48 cards. Aces rank high, followed by tens, Kings, Queens, Jacks and nines.

To win

Be the first player to reach an agreed number of points (usually 1000) over one or several deals by scoring points in declared melds and won tricks.

To deal

Cut the cards to decide the dealer. The dealer then deals out 12 cards to each player in packets of three or four.

The dealer turns up the next card to show trumps and places it face up on the table, partly obscured by the pile of stock.

High   Low

Ranking of cards in Pinochle

To score

Scores are kept on paper throughout the game. Points are awarded for melds (see below) and cards won in tricks as follows:

Melds – Class A

150 points – sequence of an Ace, ten, King, Queen and Jack of trumps (also called a "flush")

40 points – royal marriage (King and Queen of trumps)

20 points – plain, or common, marriage (King and Queen of any other suit)

Melds – Class B

40 points – Pinochle (Queen of spades and Jack of diamonds)

Melds – Class C

100 points – four Aces ("Hundred Aces")
80 points – four Kings ("Eighty Kings")
60 points – four Queens (Sixty Queens")
40 points – four Jacks ("Forty Jacks")

Tricks

At the end of the hand, points are scored for every Ace, ten, King, Queen and Jack in won tricks. Before playing, players must agree which type of scoring to follow – the modern American scoring system, or the traditional European scoring system.

Traditional scoring (European)

11 points – Ace
10 points – ten
4 points – King
3 points – Queen
2 points – Jack

Modern scoring (American)

10 points – Ace
10 points – ten
5 points – King
5 points – Queen

Points won in tricks are rounded up to the nearest multiple of ten if the units are nine, eight or seven, and rounded down to the nearest multiple of ten if the units are six and below.

Additional points

10 points – for turning up the nine of trumps at the beginning of the game
10 points – for declaring the nine of trumps, called the "dix" (pronounced "deece") during the first stage of the game (see below)
10 points – for winning the last trick of the hand

To play (first stage of the game)

Each player looks at his or her hand and works out an opening meld (see above for scoring).

The non-dealer leads with the first card of the opening trick. The dealer then plays any one of his or her cards to complete the trick. He or she does not need to follow suit. The highest leading card wins the trick unless a trump card is played. If two trump cards are played, then the highest trump wins the trick. If both players play a card of the same rank and suit, the player playing the lead card wins the trick.

Each trick is placed face down on the table in front of the player who has won it. The winner of each trick can declare a meld, placing the cards in the meld face up on the table and calling out the name of the meld and its score. Only one meld can be declared at a time.
The cards just played in a trick are discarded and each player picks up a fresh card from the pile of stock.

The cards placed on the table in a declared meld must remain there, face-up, until they are played in tricks or used to form new melds.

A player does not need to declare a meld on winning a trick.

At any point during the first stage of the game, a player holding the nine of trumps (the "dix") can declare it by laying it down on the table. He or she then scores ten points. Traditionally, the player is allowed to declare a meld at the same time. After the player wins a trick, he or she can exchange the dix for the trump card turned up under the pile of stock.

The player winning a trick and declaring a meld plays the lead card of the next trick. The game continues in this way until all the stock is used up. The players then move onto the second, and final, stage of the game.

To play (second stage of the game)

Each player takes his or her cards from the table for the last 12 tricks of the game. The winner of the previous trick leads with the next card. At this stage in the game, no melds can be declared after a trick has been won, and players must follow suit with the lead card. A player can only play a trump card if he or she cannot play a card of the same suit as the lead card. If the player cannot follow suit or play a trump, then he or she discards a card and loses the trick.

The winner of the final trick scores an extra 10 points.

At the end of the hand, points are awarded for scoring cards won in tricks and the total scores added up. If neither player has reached the 1000-point target, then the cards are re-dealt. If both players score over 1000 points in the same hand, then the cards are re-dealt and the game continues until one player reaches a score of 1250 points. If both players still draw, then the game continues until one player reaches 1500 points, and so on.

Auction Pinochle

Difficulty rating
2

Number of players
4 (with one player dealing and the other three playing against each other)

Cards
Two packs, with all cards below nine (except the Aces) removed from each pack, making a total of 48 cards.

To win
Win chips, or counters, from the other players by fulfilling a declared bid of the number of points expected to be won during the game.

To deal
The dealer deals out 15 cards to each player in five packets of three. After the first set of three cards has been dealt to each player, the dealer deals an extra three cards and leaves them face down on the table as a "widow".

To bid
Each player looks at his or her hand then, starting with the player sitting on the immediate left of the dealer, bids are made according to the number of points that each player expects to win.

The agreed starting bid is a minimum of 100 points and is usually higher, at 300 points. Players pass or bid, with bidding rising in increments of 10. Once a player has passed, he or she may not re-join the bidding.

Bidding continues until two players pass. The remaining player's bid then becomes the contract he or she has to fulfill, and the other two players usually cooperate to prevent him or her making the bid.

To play

The successful bidder takes the three widow cards from the table, shows them to the other players, and adds them to his or her hand. The player then names the trump suit and sets his or her first meld, or melds, on the table for scoring (see page 37). He or she then discards three cards, picks up any declared melds and plays the first card in the opening trick.

The bidder is allowed to change his or her mind about any displayed melds or about which cards he or she has discarded before he or she plays the first trick. If the bidder mistakenly discards a card that has been used in scoring an opening meld, he or she loses the game.

In playing tricks, the other players must follow suit if possible. If they cannot, they must play a trump card or, if they do not hold any trumps, they can discard.

If a trump card has been played on a lead card, the third player need not play a higher trump but can play a lower trump and retain the higher trump in the hope of winning a later trick. If there are two identical winning cards, then the first card played beats the second.

Only the bidder declares melds. Melds are the same for basic Pinochle. The bidder can only score 10 points for the dix (the nine of trumps) if he or she lays it on the table with his or her other melds.

To score

Melds – Class A
150 points – sequence of an Ace, ten, King, Queen and Jack of trumps
(also called a flush)
40 points – royal marriage (King and Queen of trumps)
20 points – common marriage (King and Queen of any other suit)
10 points – dix (nine of trump suit)

Melds – Class B
40 points – Pinochle (Queen of spades and Jack of diamonds)

Melds – Class C
100 points – four Aces ("Hundred Aces")
80 points – four Kings ("Eighty Kings")
60 points – four Queens ("Sixty Queens")
40 points – four Jacks ("Forty Jacks")

Tricks
The bidder scores points for any scoring cards discarded at the
beginning of the game. He or she also scores an additional 10 points
for winning the last trick.

As with standard Pinochle, players must agree whether to follow the
modern or traditional scoring system for cards in won tricks:

Traditional scoring (European)
11 points – Ace
10 points – ten
4 points – King
3 points – Queen
2 points – Jack

Modern scoring (American)
10 points – Ace
10 points – ten
5 points – King
5 points – Queen

To win chips
Each game consists of one hand. The bidder wins chips, or counters, from the other players depending on whether or not he or she has made the declared bid. For example:

Points bid	Number of chips won from each of the other players
300–340	3
350–390	5
400–440	10
450–490	15
500–540	20
550–590	25
600 plus	30

To run a kitty
In most games of Auction Pinochle, players set up a kitty. Each player must pay three chips into the kitty at the beginning of each game and again if all three players pass during bidding.

If a bidder fails to fulfil a declared bid of 350 points or more, he or she must pay into the kitty and pay the other players as well. If the bidder succeeds in fulfilling a declared bid of 350 points or more, he or she can collect from the kitty as well as from the other players.

Partnership-Auction Pinochle

Auction Pinochle can also be played with four players playing in partnerships. Partners sit opposite one another at the table. Play is the same as for Auction Pinochle with each partnership aiming to score 1000 points or more over several deals. Players bid according to the minimum number of points they expect to score in their partnerships, starting with the player sitting to the left of the dealer. Once three players pass, the player making the last bid secures the contract and names the trump suit.

The bidding partnership counts its score first. If the partnership fulfilled its bid, it scores any points made. If the partnership didn't make its bid, then the amount of the bid is subtracted from the partnership's total score. The non-bidding partnership also scores for any points made. However, if it does not win a single trick, it scores nothing.

Brag

This popular bluffing game is one of several ancestors of Poker. Unlike Poker, which is played with five cards, Brag is played with three, six or nine cards and the highest winning combination is three of a kind, or three cards of the same rank.

Three-Card Brag

Difficulty rating
2

Number of players
3–7 players

Cards
52

To win
Stay in the game long enough to win the kitty by bluffing or holding the best hand.

To deal
Cards are shuffled before the first deal of the game but are not shuffled again until the start of the next game unless one hand is won on a prial (three of a kind).

Players take it in turn to deal with the deal passing to the left around the table. Cards just played in a hand are gathered up and put at the bottom of the pack. A game ends when each player has had a turn dealing the cards. The dealer deals three cards one at a time and face down to each player.

Sometimes (particularly when there are five players or fewer), each player may be required to ante one chip or counter into the kitty in the centre of the table before the first deal of the game.

Brag hands

Brag hands are as follows, from high to low:

• A prial or three of a kind. Although Aces are high, the best prial is a prial of threes, followed by Aces, then Kings, down to twos.

• A running flush (three cards of the same suit in a sequence).

• A run (three cards of different suits in a sequence). Again, although Aces are high, the best run or running flush is Ace - two - three followed by Ace - King - Queen, and so on, down to two - three - four.

• A flush (three cards of the same suit).

• A pair (two cards of the same rank).

• A "high" – one card simply being the highest in the hand. The lowest possible Brag hand is therefore a two, three and five of different suits.

A higher Brag hand beats a lower Brag hand, with a hand holding a pair being the lowest. If two hands are the same, then the hand containing the highest card wins, or the second-highest card if the highest cards in each hand are the same.

Lowest Brag hand – one card simply a "high"

Ace high

Five high

Pair – Two cards of the same rank with the third card unmatched

Highest pair

Lowest pair

Flush – three cards of the same suit

Highest flush

Lowest flush

Run – three
cards in a
sequence
(not the
same suit)

Highest run   Lowest run

Running
flush – three
cards in a
sequence
(the same
suit)

Highest running flush   Lowest running flush

Prial
(highest
Brag hand)
– three
cards of the
same rank –
the highest
Brag hand

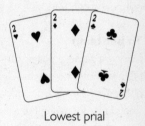

Highest prial   Lowest prial

To play

After looking at his or her hand, each player in turn, starting with the player to the immediate left of the dealer, either drops out or makes a bet on his or her hand by putting one or more chips into the kitty.

Each bet must be either the same as that made by the previous player or no more than an amount agreed at the beginning of the game.

Play continues with players dropping out when they decide not to increase the ante until only two players remain in the game.

The last two players can either continue to raise the ante until one drops out of the game (in which case the remaining player wins the whole kitty), or one player can "see" the other's cards. To do this, he or she has to pay twice the amount of the last stake. Both players then show their cards and the highest brag hand (see illustration) wins the kitty.

In Brag, a person with an inferior hand but with the ability and confidence to bluff can cause the holder of better hands to fold and drop out of the game, so the player with the best Brag hand does not necessarily win.

To bet blind

During a game, a player can leave his or her hand face down on the table without looking at it and "bet blind". While doing this, he or she only pays half the amount put into the kitty by the previous player. The player following the player betting blind must pay double the amount staked by that player.

If one of the last two players in a hand is betting blind, then the player not betting blind can only pay to "see" the cards of the other player after that player has looked at them.

To cover the kitty

In some games of Brag, it is allowed for a player to "cover the kitty" during a game if he or she wishes to stay in the game but has run out of chips, or counters.

To cover the kitty, the player simply lays his or her hand face down on top of it. The other players remaining in the game then start a new kitty and continue to play. The winner of the hand wins the new kitty then compares his or her hand with that of the player covering the original kitty. The player with the best Brag hand of the two then wins the original kitty.

Brag Variations

Brag may be played with wild cards – either the twos, or a Joker added to the pack. Wild cards can be used to represent any other card to make up a good Brag hand. If two hands are equal but one hand contains one or more wild cards, then the hand containing no or fewer wild cards wins.

Five-Card Brag

Five-card Brag is played in exactly the same way as three-card Brag except that five cards are dealt to each player, singly, at the beginning of the game. Each player then discards two cards to leave him or her with the best possible hand.

By agreement at the start of the game, a prial of fives becomes the best hand rather than a prial of threes.

Seven-Card Brag

In seven-card Brag, as with other variations, a prial of sevens is usually the best hand rather than a prial of threes. (This must be agreed at the beginning of the game.)

Before the cards are dealt, each player puts the same stake into the kitty. Seven cards are then dealt to each player. If any player has four cards of the same rank in his or her hand, then the player wins the kitty and the cards are re-dealt. If not, each player makes up the two best-possible Brag hands with three cards in each and discards the seventh card. Both hands are then placed face down on the table in front of each player, with the higher hand to the player's left and the lower hand to the player's right.

The player to the immediate left of the dealer turns up his left hand first and each player either passes or turns up his or her own left hand if it beats the first hand. After each player has had a turn, then the player with the highest left hand turns his or her right hand face up.

Play continues in the same way around the table with each player either passing or turning up his or her right hand if it beats all the other right hands.

Nine-Card Brag

In nine-card Brag, the unbeatable prial is either a prial of nines or a prial of threes which should be agreed at the beginning of the game. Play is the same as for seven-card Brag except that each player is dealt nine cards and must arrange them into three Brag hands. The hands are placed on the table, with the highest on the left and the lowest on the right. A player can only take the whole kitty if all three of his or her hands wins.

Bridge

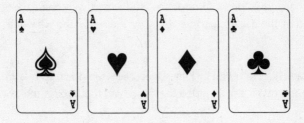

Bridge was derived from Whist in the late 1800s. There are several forms of Bridge but the most widely played version is Contract Bridge, the basics of which are described in this section. The auction or bidding in Bridge requires considerable skill to play well but whole books have been written on the subject and there are plenty of Bridge clubs and classes all over the country for anyone keen to learn more!

Contract Bridge

Difficulty rating
3

Number of players
4, played in partnerships with partners sitting opposite each other and being called north-south and east-west.

Cards
52 (although two packs of cards are usually used, with one pack being shuffled by the dealer's partner ready for the next hand while the other is dealt).

Aces rank high, followed by King, Queen, Jack, ten down to two. In Bridge, the two is usually called the deuce and the three is the trey.

Points are also awarded for "honours".

When playing "no trumps", the honours are the four Aces. When there are trumps, the honours are the Ace, King, Queen, Jack and ten of the trump suit.

Ranking of cards in Bridge.

Honours cards at "no trumps"

To win

Gain the most points over the course of three games, called a "rubber". Each game is won by the first partnership to score 100 points "below the line" on the scoresheet (see below), and the first partnership to win two games wins the rubber.

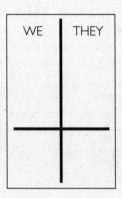

In Contract Bridge, scores are kept on a scoring pad, with scores on individual players' hands being written above the line ("game going" scores), and penalty or bonus points being written above the line.

To deal

Partners are decided before the deal, either by agreement or by cutting the pack of cards with the players drawing the two highest cards playing against those drawing the two lowest.

The first dealer is the player holding the highest cut card. If two players draw cards of the same rank, then the cards are ranked by suit with spades being the highest, followed by hearts, diamonds then clubs.

The dealer usually invites the player sitting on his or her left to cut the pack, then deals out all the cards one by one and face down, starting with the player on his or her left, so each player has 13 cards.

To bid

Each player picks up and looks at his or her cards then bids according to the number of tricks his or her partnership plans to win over during the course of the game either with or without trumps.

Bids are always made in excess of six (the "book") so a bid of "One spades" means a player plans his or her partnership to take seven tricks (the book of six plus one extra) with spades as the trump suit. Similarly, a bid of "Three, hearts" means a player and his or her partner plans to take nine tricks with hearts as the chosen trump suit.

During the bidding, each suit has a ranking. Spades is the highest ranked suit, followed by hearts, diamonds then clubs. A bid of "One spades" is therefore greater than a bid of "One hearts" and a bid of "One hearts" is greater than a bid of "One diamonds". Bidding "One clubs" is therefore the lowest bid of all.

The highest bid is one to play "no trumps" which means the player plans to win a certain number of tricks without any trump suit.

The highest bid of all is "Seven no trumps" (also known as a grand slam) meaning that a player plans his or her partnership to take all 13 tricks in the hand.

Here are some examples of sample bids, from lowest to highest.

- One clubs
- One diamonds
- One hearts
- One spades
- Two clubs
- Two diamonds
- Two hearts
- Two spades
- Three clubs

- Three diamonds
- Three hearts
- Three spades

and so on up to

- Six clubs
- Six diamonds
- Six hearts
- Six spades
- Six no trumps (small slam)
- Seven clubs
- Seven diamonds
- Seven hearts
- Seven spades
- Seven no trumps (grand slam)

During the bidding, a player may do one of the following:
- Bid, with each bid made having to be higher than the last bid.
- Pass, meaning that the player does not wish to bid (although the player can make another bid later)
- Double
- Redouble

If all four players pass during the first round of the bidding, then the cards are shuffled and re-dealt, with the deal passing to the player sitting to the left of the original dealer.

Once three players say "pass" after a bid, double or redouble then the bidding ends and the last bid becomes the contract for the game.

A bid of "double" means the player thinks he or she can prevent the previous bid being made if it becomes the contract. If the double becomes the contract (by being followed by three "passes" rather than a higher bid), then the scores are doubled for the partnership if it fulfils its bid or doubled for the other partnerhip (that is, the partnerhip that called double) if the bidding partnership does not fulfil its bid.

If a player bids "double" then the next player can bid "redouble", which means he or she is resasserting confidence in his or her partner's previous bid. A redoubled bid can be outbid by any player making a higher call to win more tricks or to win the same number of tricks with a higher-ranking suit.

The partnership making the highest accepted call must try to fulfil the contract during the play and the other partnership tries to prevent it.

To play

The member of a partnership who made the declaration of a trump suit or "no trumps" is called the "declarer" and he or she plays both hands of the partnership during the game. His partner, called the "dummy", lays his or her cards face up on the table as soon as the lead card has been played in the first trick and takes no further part in the game for that hand.

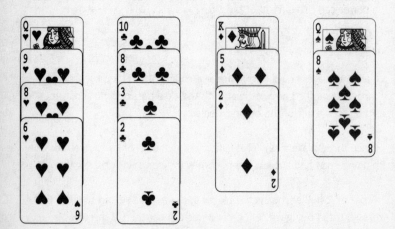

The dummy hand is laid out on the table facing the dealer. Cards are arranged in suits, with trumps on the left (as seen by the declarer).

The player sitting to the immediate left of the declarer leads with the first card of the opening trick. Play continues clockwise around the table with the declarer playing cards from the dummy hand then his or her own, in turn. The winner of a trick plays the lead card of the following trick until all 13 tricks have been played and won.

Play is the same as in Whist in that each player must follow suit with the lead card if possible. If a player is unable to follow suit, he or she can play a trump or discard. The highest card in the leading suit or the highest trump card (if played) wins the trick.

Won tricks should be placed face down on the table in front of the declarer and one of the players in the opposing partnership, arranged at right angles to each other and slightly overlapping so they can be counted easily.

Once the bidding partnership has won six tricks, it is said to have "made the book". The tricks in the book are usually put in one pile so that tricks over the book can be clearly counted.

To score
Both partnerships usually keep the score during the game to settle any disputes that may arise.

If a partnership wins one game out of the rubber it is described as "vulnerable". This means it can gain more points for successful bids and lose more points for unsuccessful bids. If each partnership has won one game, then both are said to be vulnerable.

WE	THEY	
60		
	30	
100		Above the line bonus
	100	points for overtricks,
	30	holding honours and
60		taking the rubber
100		
500		
70		
	60	First game
30		
	120	Second game
40		Third game –
100		WE wins rubber

Scores are written either above the line or below the line on the scoring sheet, depending on the type of score. In this sample scoresheet, WE won the third game over six deals and received 500 bonus points for taking the rubber. Other bonus points for overtricks and holding honours are written above the line.

Score for the bidders (if the bid is fulfilled)

	Score	Doubled	Redoubled
Below the line			
For every contracted trick over book			
– with a minor suit as trumps (clubs or diamonds)	20	40	80
– with a major suit as trumps (hearts or spades)	30	60	120
– with no trumps (for first trick)	40	80	160
– with no trumps (for subsequent tricks)	30	60	120
Above the line (non-vulnerable)			
For every extra trick (overtrick) above contract			
– with a minor suit as trumps	20	100	200
– with a major suit as trumps	30	100	200
– with no trumps	30	100	200
Above the line (vulnerable)			
For every extra trick (overtrick) above contract			
– with a minor suit as trumps	20	200	400
– with a major suit as trumps	30	200	400
– with no trumps	30	200	400
Above the line bonus points			
– Fulfilling a double or redouble	50		
– Making a small slam (non-vulnerable)	500		
– Making a small slam (vulnerable)	750		
– Making a grand slam (non-vulnerable)	1000		
– Making a grand slam (vulnerable)	1500		

Score for the non-bidders (if bid is not fulfilled)

	Score	Doubled	Redoubled
Above the line (non-vulnerable)			
– For every trick (undertrick) less than contract	50	-	-
– For first undertrick	-	100	200
– For subsequent undertricks	-	200	400
Above the line (vulnerable)			
– For every trick (undertrick) less than contract	100	-	-
– For first undertrick	-	200	400
– For subsequent undertricks	-	300	600

Bonuses (awarded to either partnership)

Above the line for held honours

– Four trump honours held in one hand before play	100
– Five trump honours held in one hand before play	150
– Four Aces held in one hand (no trumps) before play	150

Above the line for rubbers

– Winning rubber in two games	700
– Winning rubber in three games	500
– For one game won in an unfinished rubber	300
– For a partscore in an unfinished rubber	50

If a declaring partnership fulfils its contract, it scores below the line for every trick bid and won and above the line for overtricks and bonuses. If it does not make its bid, the defenders score above the line for undertricks. Both sides score points for having held "honours" before the play begins.

The first partnership to win 100 or more trick points wins a game over one or more deals.

A partnership receives 700 bonus points for winning two games straight (when the opposing partnerhip has not won one), and 500 bonus points for winning two games when the opposing partnership has won one game.

The rubber is won by the partnership with the highest total of trick and bonus points.

Cassino

Cassino is an old Italian game which is mostly played by two players but can work well for three players or for four playing in partnerships. It demands a reasonable memory and good powers of concentration.

Basic Cassino

Difficulty rating
2

Number of players
2–3 (but best for two players)

Cards
52, with cards having no ranking but with number cards counting at their face value (Ace counting as one, two counting as two, and so on). Court cards (Jack, Queen and King) have no face value.

To win
Score the most points by capturing the most cards.

To deal
The cards are cut to determine the first dealer, with the player cutting the lowest card dealing first.

On the first deal, two cards are dealt face down to the non-dealer, two cards are dealt face up on the table, then two cards are dealt to the dealer. Then a further two cards are dealt to non-dealer, table and dealer, so that each player has four cards and there are four cards face up on the table.

(If three are playing, then two cards are dealt to each player, two to the table, two more to each player then the last two to the table.)

When each player has played all four of his or her cards, the same dealer deals out another four cards to each player, again in sets of two, but none this time to the table. Subsequent deals continue in this way with the same dealer dealing out the cards until there are no cards left in the stock or in either hand.

When all the cards have been used up, the other player deals the cards for the next round. There are six rounds in a game, with each player taking it in turns to deal.

To play
Playing one card at a time, each player takes it in turns to try to capture cards that lie face up on the table by pairing them or by "building" them so that they can be captured. Any captured cards are placed face down on the table in front of each player.

If a player cannot use a card to capture another card (or cards) when it is his or her turn to play, then he or she must "trail" one of the cards in the hand, by laying it face up on the table. Any trailed cards remain face up on the table and can be captured or used for building on by either player.

To capture cards
Cards are captured in several ways (see page 66), with points being awarded for capturing the most cards, the most spades, the most Aces, the ten of diamonds and the two of spades (see "To score" page 71).

When capturing a card, a player usually puts the card from his or her hand face down on top of the captured card and pulls both cards towards him or her. The cards remain in a pile, face down, except when a player makes a sweep (see page 68), in which case the cards in the sweep must remain face up for scoring.

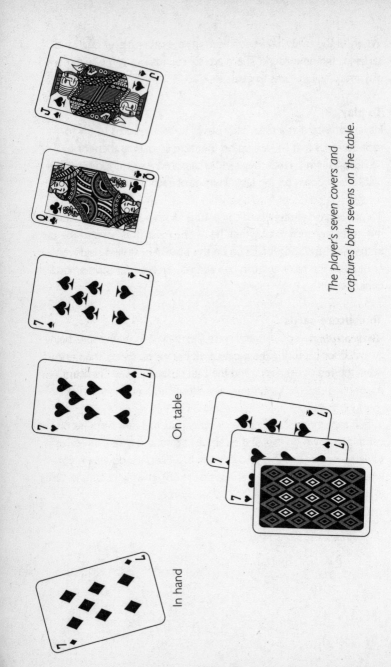

On table

In hand

The player's seven covers and captures both sevens on the table.

By pairing

The simplest way of capturing a card is by pairing it. For example, a player can capture a single card on the table with a single card in his or her hand, so a Queen can capture a Queen, and a two can capture a two, and so on.

Cards from an Ace through to a ten can capture more than one card at a time depending on how many there are on the table. For example, a player holding a six can capture two sixes at the same time if there are two sixes on the table, or three sixes if there are three sixes on the table.

A picture card can either capture a pair or make a group of all four, so a Queen can either capture one Queen or three Queens, but not two because capturing two would mean that one single Queen would remain unpaired.

By grouping

A group of cards can be captured by a single card if the numerical value of the group adds up to the value of the card in the hand. For example a ten can capture a five, a three and a two. It could also capture another ten if there happened to be one because it would make a pair.

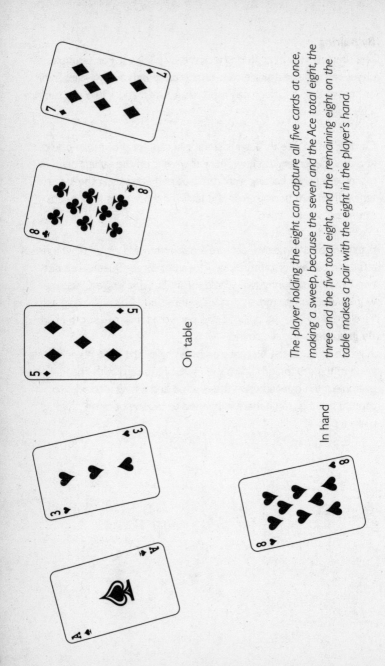

On table

In hand

The player holding the eight can capture all five cards at once, making a sweep, because the seven and the Ace total eight, the three and the five total eight, and the remaining eight on the table makes a pair with the eight in the player's hand.

By building

Cards can also be captured by "leaving a build". For example, if there is a six on the table and a player holds a nine and a three, then he or she can place the three on the six and say "building nine" with the intention of capturing the "build" (the three and six combined) with the nine the next time round.

If a player places a card on the table and does not say what number he or she is building, then his or her opponent can separate the cards and capture them if possible with his or her own cards.

By duplicating a build

Additional cards can be captured by duplicating a build. For example, if a player is "building nine" and his or her opponent trails a seven, then if the first player also holds a two, he or she can put the seven on the table alongside the six and the three, add his or her two, and therefore duplicate the build. The player would then take both builds with the nine next time round.

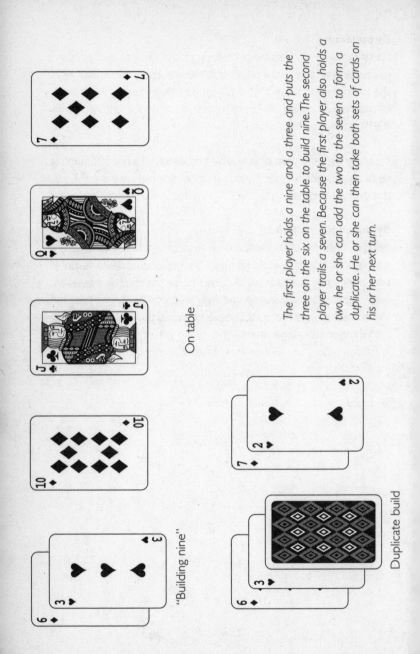

On table

"Building nine"

Duplicate build

The first player holds a nine and a three and puts the three on the six on the table to build nine. The second player trails a seven. Because the first player also holds a two, he or she can add the two to the seven to form a duplicate. He or she can then take both sets of cards on his or her next turn.

By increasing a build

Builds can be built higher by adding other cards. For example, if one player has placed a three on top of a five and has said "building eight", then the other player can add an Ace on top of the three and five and say "building nine", assuming he or she holds a nine as well as an Ace and is therefore able to capture the cards on his or her next turn.

Players can only increase on a single build, not a build that has been duplicated. Builds can only be increased by using cards in the hand, not by using cards already on the table.

Once a player has started a build, he or she must capture it, duplicate it, or increase it the next time it is his or her turn to play. Players are not allowed to start a build and then trail a card or capture another card or group of cards at their next turn.

When all the cards in the stock have been used up, any cards remaining face up on the table are claimed by the player who has made the last capture and each player then counts his or her score according to his or her captured cards.

To score

Points are awarded as follows:

3 points – for capturing 27 or more cards
2 points – for capturing the ten of diamonds ("big cassino")
1 point – for capturing the two of spades ("little cassino")
1 point – for capturing each Ace
1 point – for capturing seven or more spades
1 point – for a sweep

The first player to get the most points in the round or the first player to reach a total of 21 or more points over several rounds wins the game.

Spade Cassino

Spade Cassino is played in exactly the same way as Cassino except that spades score additional points as follows:

2 points – for capturing the Jack of spades
2 points – for capturing the two of spades ("little cassino")
1 point – for capturing each of the other spades.

The first player to get the most points in a round or the first player to reach a total of 61 or more points over several rounds wins the game. Scores are either kept on paper or on a cribbage board (see page 77).

Royal Cassino

Royal Cassino is played in the same way as Cassino except that players can capture face, or royal, cards as well as cards from one to ten and use them to build.

In Royal Cassino, the court cards count as follows:
Jacks – 11 points each
Queens – 12 points each
Kings – 13 points each
Aces can count as 1 or as 14 (to be agreed)
In addition, "big cassino" can count as either 10 or 16 points, and "little cassino" as 2 or 15 points.

Royal Draw Cassino

Royal Draw Cassino is the same as Royal Cassino with the players being able to capture and build on face cards. The main difference is that instead of each player using up all four cards in his or her hand and then dealing out four more, each player draws one card from the top of the pile of stock every time he or she plays or trails a card. When the cards in the stock have been used up, the play continues in the same way as that for basic Cassino.

Cribbage

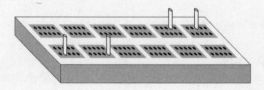

Cribbage is an English game that was thought to have been developed by the poet and courtier Sir John Suckling in the early 1600s. It was once played mainly by the aristocracy but is now mostly played in pubs. The game requires a quick mind and reasonable maths skills, and is best played with two players.

Cribbage

Difficulty rating
2

Number of players
2 (although three and four can play with variations)

Cards
52, with Aces ranking high

To win
Be the first player to reach 61 or 121 points.

To keep score
Scores can be kept on paper but traditionally a cribbage board is used to keep count.

To deal
The players cut the deck to determine the first dealer with the player cutting the lower card dealing first. Starting with the non-dealer, the dealer deals out six cards each, face down and one at a time.

After dealing, each player looks at his or her hand, keeps the best combination for scoring, and discards two cards, placing them face down on the table near the dealer. These four cards form the crib and they are used at the end of the game to make up the dealer's total score.

The non-dealer then cuts the remaining cards and the dealer turns up the top card. This card is placed face up as the "start" card.

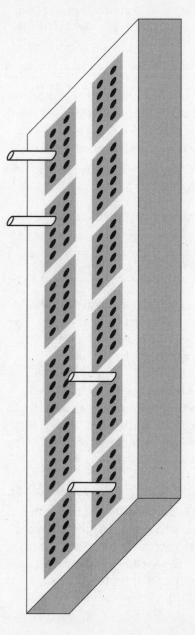

Each player pegs his or her score on the cribbage board. Each hole pegged counts as one point. Players usually use two pegs each, with both pegs being moved along the outer row of holes first then back along the inner row. Pegs are moved alternately, so that each player can clearly see what score has just been pegged. For example, if a player scores two points, he or she moves the first peg two holes on the board. If he or she then scores a further eight points, he or she moves the second peg eight holes beyond the first peg, showing the last pegged score (eight) and the total score (ten). Pegs are leapfrogged in this way until one player reaches or exceeds the winning score of 61 (up and down the board once plus the centre "game hole" or 121 (up and down the board twice).

If the start card is a Jack, the dealer can immediately peg two points "for his heels", as long as he or she does this before the first card is played.

To play

The non-dealer places one card from his or her hand face up on the table, announcing its face value. Following the card that has just been played, the dealer then plays one card from his or her hand and places it in a separate pile on the table, announcing both the combined face value with the other player's card, and its scoring value (see "To score during play" opposite.)

Cards are kept in separate piles for additional scoring at the end of the hand. However, cards are considered together for scoring while the hand is being played.

To keep count

Players keep count as they play according to the cards' face value. In keeping count, Aces count as one, court cards count as 10, and all other cards count at their face value. The count of 31 points is the maximum total value of all cards allowed in play at a time.

When a player cannot play his or her next card without exceeding the allowed total value of 31 points (for example, if the count is at 22 and the player holds a court card with a face value of 10) then he or she calls "go" and the other player gets another turn, or turns, until he or she is also unable to play without the total exceeding 31.

At this point, the round ends and another round begins, still using the four cards dealt at the beginning of the game. The first card of the new round is started by the player who did not play the last card in the previous round. If the cards in play total 31 before all the cards in the first hand have been used up, then another round is started, until each player has played all four cards in his or her hand.

To score during play

During play, each player tries to peg as many points as possible for scoring combinations of cards. Points are awarded and pegged on the cribbage board for the following combinations:

2 points – for a pair
6 points – for three of a kind (sometimes called a pair royal)
12 points – for four of a kind (sometimes called a double pair royal)
2 points – for any combination of two or more cards that totals 15
3 points – for playing the third card in a run
4 points – for playing the fourth card in a run
4 points – for holding four cards of the same suit in a hand (only scored during the show)
5 points – for five cards of the same suit using the start card (only scored during the show)

1 point – for "go" (playing the last card in a round that reaches less than 31 points)
2 points – for playing the last card when the count reaches exactly 31 points
1 point – for "last", or playing the last card in a hand

Players can score points for runs even if the cards in the run are not played in consecutive order. For example, if the first player plays a six and the second player plays a five, then the first player can play a seven and score three points for a run of three cards. If the second player has a four, then he or she can play it and count four points for a run of four cards, and so on.

Players can also score for different winning combinations at the same time. For example, if the cards in play run four then six and the next player plays a five, he or she scores two points for the 15 and a further two points for a run of three cards, pegging a combined total of four on the cribbage board.

To call

Announcing total values of cards and scoring combinations follows a certain style, as follows:

Player	Card played	Announces	Pegged score
First player	3	3	-
Second player	4	7	-
First player	4	11 and 2 for a pair	2
Second player	4	"Fifteen two" and 6 for three 4s (or "fifteen two" and 6 for a pair royal)	8

Play continues until the last card of a hand is played, with its player getting an extra pegged point "one for last".

To score during the show

When the players have played all four cards of the first hand, each player "shows" all the different scoring combinations he or she can make with the four cards in his or her hand plus the start card, starting with the non-dealer.

The dealer then scores his or her own cards, then the four cards in the crib. The dealer then adds the crib score to his or her own score and pegs it on the board.

Both players are allowed to use the start card in their show of cards.

For example, if the face up card is the seven of clubs, and a player's hand contains the seven of spades, the eight of diamonds, the nine of hearts and the nine of clubs, then the player could score as follows:

2 points – for a pair (the two nines)

2 points – for a pair (the two sevens)

2 points – for a fifteen (the seven of clubs and the eight of diamonds)

2 points – for a fifteen (the seven of spades and the eight of diamonds)

12 points – for four separate runs of three cards valued at three points each:
the seven of clubs with the eight and the nine of hearts, the seven of clubs with the eight and the nine of diamonds, plus the seven of spades with the eight and each of the nines

20 points pegged in total

In another example, if a player holds the Queen of diamonds, the Queen of hearts, a Jack of clubs and a five and the start card is a ten of clubs, then he or she could score:

2 points – for a pair (the two Queens)

1 point   – for the Jack ("his nobs")

6 points – for two different runs of three cards (ten, Jack, Queen of diamonds and ten, Jack, Queen of hearts)

8 points – for "fifteen two" four times – the five with each of the court cards and the ten

17 points pegged in total

The play continues in this way, with new deals after each round, until the first player reaches a total of 61 or 121 points. (Note: If a player is nearing the winning total, it can be an advantage to be the non-dealer and have the first show.)

Cribbage Variations

In some variations of cribbage, if a player fails to notice a scoring combination, the other player can call out "muggins" and peg the score for himself.

Cribbage for Three Players

Cribbage can be played with three players. The game is played in exactly the same way as cribbage for two except that each player is dealt five cards instead of six, one card is dealt to the crib and the players discard one card each into the crib. As with two-hand cribbage, the winner is the first player to reach a score of 121 points.

Cribbage for Four Players

Four players can either play solo, playing in the same way as for two-hand cribbage, or in partnerships. Partners face each other across the table. Each player's score is earned individually but scores are pegged as a partnership.

Five-card Cribbage

Cribbage can also be played with two players each being dealt five or seven cards. The game is played in the same way as six-card cribbage with slight differences in scoring, as follows:

Five-card

• The player who does not deal the first hand pegs three points before the start of play announced "three for last" as compensation for the dealer being able to score on the first crib.

• The winner is the first player to reach 61 points (not 121).

Seven-card

Each player is dealt seven cards each and discards two into the crib. The winner is the first player to reach 181 points.

Ecarté

Ecarté (meaning "discarded") is a game for two players, which was popular during the 19th century. Although quick to learn, it requires skill in deciding when to exchange cards and when to play a hand. Several games are derived from Ecarté, the best-known being the US game of Euchre, and the UK game Napoleon, or Nap.

Ecarté

Difficulty rating
2

Number of players
2

Cards
32, with all the cards below seven (except the Aces) removed from the pack

High   Low

Ranking of cards in Ecarté

To win
Be the first player to win five points.

To deal
Each player cuts the cards to determine the first dealer. The dealer deals five cards face down starting with the other player in packets of three, then two.

The next card from the stock is then turned up for trumps. If that card is a King, the dealer immediately scores one point. If the non-dealer holds the King of trumps, then he or she can also gain one point if he or she chooses to declare it to the other player.

To exchange cards
If the non-dealer wants to draw new cards from the stock to improve his or her hand, he or she says "propose". If the dealer agrees to an exchange of cards, he or she says "accept" to accept the proposal.

If a player is happy with his or her cards, he or she says "play" and neither player makes an exchange.

To exchange cards, the non-dealer discards one or more cards face down and picks up the same number from the stock. The dealer then exchanges one or more of his or her cards. The non-dealer then gets another chance to "propose" or "play" and so on until the dealer wants no further exchanges and calls "play".

Players are not allowed to exchange cards if they hold cards that could win at least three tricks.

To play
The non-dealer leads the first trick by playing the first card, face up. The dealer must follow suit if possible or play a trump card. If he or she does not have a trump, then any card can be played. Tricks are won by the highest card of the leading suit, a trump card if played onto a lead card, or the highest trump card if the lead card is a trump.

The winner of a trick plays the first card of the next trick and so on, until all five cards have been played.

To score
Points are scored as follows:
1 point – winning three or four tricks
2 points – winning all five tricks (called a "vole")
1 point – awarded to the dealer if the turn-up is a King or to the player who holds the King of the trump suit (but only if declared before playing the first trick)
1 point – awarded to one player if the other does not win at least three tricks after refusing to make an exchange of cards.

The first player to reach five points wins the game over as many deals as necessary.

Non-dealer

"Propose"

X   X

↓   ↓

"Propose"

Turn-up (spades
are trumps)

X   X

↓   ↓

"Propose"

Non-dealer's hand

Dealer

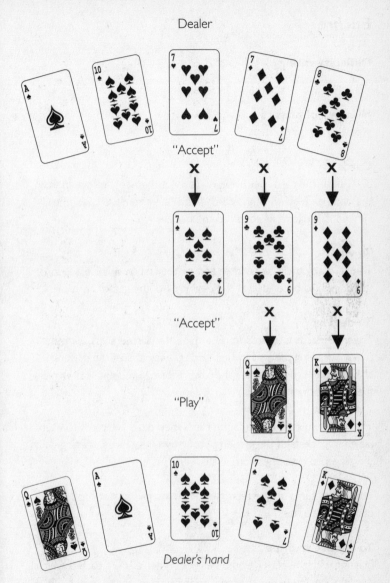

The dealer accepts the non-dealer's first two proposes to exchange cards but decides to play when securing the Queen. The dealer's cards are stronger and he or she ends up winning three tricks to two.

Euchre

Difficulty rating
2

Number of players
4, playing in partnerships

Cards
32, with all the cards below seven (except the Aces) removed from the pack; or 24, with all the cards below eight removed. In some variations, the Joker is added to the pack as well.

To win
Take as many tricks as possible and be the first to win five, seven, or ten points (to be agreed at the beginning of the game).

To deal
The players cut the cards to determine the partnerships, with the players drawing the two lowest cards playing against the players drawing the highest cards. If the Joker is being used and is drawn, then the player draws again.

The dealer shuffles and cuts the cards then deals five cards to each player in packets of three then two, or two then three, starting with the player to his or her immediate left.

The dealer turns up the next card from the pile of stock to determine trumps.

To choose trumps
Starting with the player to the dealer's immediate left, each player has the opportunity of either accepting the turn-up as the trump suit (saying "I order it up") or passing. Players also state whether they intend to play "alone" or "assist" their partners.

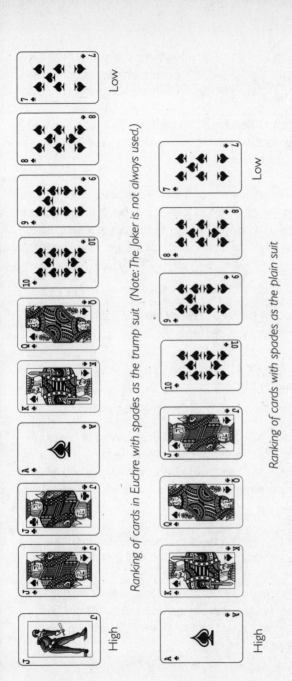

Ranking of cards in Euchre with spades as the trump suit (Note: The Joker is not always used.)

Ranking of cards with spades as the plain suit

In the trump suit, the Jack is the highest card (unless the Joker is being used) and is called the "Right Bower", followed by the Jack of the same-colour suit (the "Left Bower"), then the Ace, King, Queen, ten, nine, eight and seven. In the other suits, Aces rank high. (There will be no Jack in the suit that is the same colour as the trump suit as it becomes a high-ranking trump card.) Playing with the Joker is optional. If it is used, it becomes the highest trump and is called the "Best Bower".

As soon as a player "orders up" or accepts the trump, play begins and the dealer has the option of discarding one card from his or her hand face down on the table and taking up the turned-up trump.

If all four players pass, the turn-up is turned face down and a second round of bidding starts. Each player can now either pass again or name a different suit as trump.

Bids are either choosing the suit of the same colour as the original turn-up (called "making it next"), or choosing either of the suits of the other colour (called "crossing it"). The bidder does not need to state exactly which suit he or she chooses (although if it is "make it next", then it is obvious). Once again, each player also chooses to play alone or assist.

If a bid is made during the second round the dealer cannot exchange one of his or her cards because there is no turn-up card on the table.

If all four players pass for a second time, then the cards are re-dealt, with the deal passing to the left.

To play
If the winning bidder has chosen to play alone, then his or her partner lays his or her cards face down on the table before the first trick and does not take part in the hand. In this case, the lead card of the first trick is played by the player sitting to the immediate left of the solo player.

If the players are playing in partnerships, then the first card of the lead trick is played by the player sitting to the left of the dealer.

The other players have to play a card of the same suit if possible. If they cannot follow suit, they can play a trump card or discard. The trick is won by the highest lead card or by the highest trump card if trumps card is played.

The winner of each trick plays the lead card of the following trick.

The player or partnership choosing trumps aims to take at least three tricks, with the other players aiming to "euchre" or stop them.

To score
In simple scoring, the player choosing trumps and his or her partner wins the hand and the game if they make at least three tricks. If they do not, they are "euchred" and lose.

To increase the length of a game, points can be awarded, with the first partnership to reach five, seven, or ten points (as agreed) winning the game over as many deals as necessary.

Points are awarded as follows:
1 point – for taking three or four tricks
2 points – for winning all five tricks (called a "march")
4 points – for playing solo and winning the march (all five tricks)
2 points – to the opponents if a partnership fails to win three tricks

Three-handed Euchre
Euchre can also be played by three players in a game sometimes called "Cut-throat Euchre". In three-handed Euchre, the player making trumps always plays alone against the other two players who play in a partnership to try to euchre the solo player. Scoring is the same as for partnership Euchre except that the player scores three points for winning all five tricks, not four points.

Five Hundred

Five Hundred is a member of the Euchre family of card games and is a particularly good game for three or five players. Although it was devised in the United States as a spin-off from Euchre around 100 years ago, it gradually became supplanted by other games there. However, it has since become one of the most popular card games in Australia, where it is often played with special "500" packs of 63 cards, which contain a Joker, elevens and twelves in all four suits, plus two red thirteens.

Five Hundred

Difficulty rating
2

Number of players
3 (but it can also be played with 2, 4, 5 or 6 players – see end of section)

Cards
32, with all the cards below seven (except the Aces) removed from the pack. A Joker is often added as the top trump.

To win
Be the first player to reach 500 points.

To deal
The players cut the cards to determine the first dealer, with the King ranking highest, the Joker the lowest and Ace second-lowest. The player with the lowest cut card deals first.

The dealer deals out 10 cards to each player, starting with the player to his or her left. The cards are dealt face down in sets – either in packets of three, two, three, two; or in three packets of three followed by one final card.

The three remaining cards are placed face down on the table.

To make a bid
Each player looks at his or her cards then takes it in turns to make a bid or "pass", starting with the player to the left of the dealer. If a player passes, he or she cannot bid again in that hand.

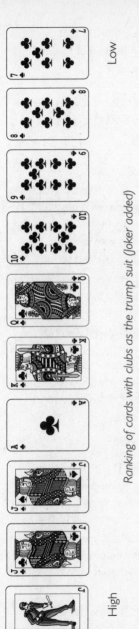

Ranking of cards with clubs as the trump suit (Joker added)

Ranking of cards with clubs as a plain suit

Ranking of cards in Five Hundred in a game for three players. The added Joker becomes the highest card in the trump suit, followed by the Jack of trumps (called the "Right Bower") and the Jack of the same colour suit (the "Left Bower").

Each bid states the trump suit and the number of tricks that the player expects to win with the hand (with a minimum of six), and each bid must be higher than the previous bid.

In Five Hundred, each suit has a ranking. Spades is the lowest, followed by clubs, diamonds, hearts, then "no trumps" (bidding to play the hand without a trump suit).

The lowest possible bid is therefore "six spades" (six tricks with spades as the trump suit) and the highest is "10 no trumps" (ten tricks without any suit as trumps) – see the scoring figures on page 99 for the value of other bids. Sometimes, players make their bids according to the value of the game, such as "40" (six tricks with spades as trumps) or "160" (seven tricks with clubs as trumps), and so on.

Players can also bid to lose every trick in the hand, playing with no trump suit (called "misère") or lose every trick with no trump suit and playing with their cards face up on the table (open misère).

The player with the highest bid wins the contract for the hand and must try to fulfil it. The winner picks up the face-down cards on the table and, if he or she likes, can play with one or more of them, discarding the same number from his or her hand.

To play
The bidder plays the lead card of the first trick. The other players (with the play going clockwise from left to right) must follow suit if possible or play a card from another suit.

In a three-player game, the two non-bidders play in a loose partnership to try to prevent the bidder from winning his or her bid. However, each player scores separately for his or her own tricks.

A trick is won by the highest card of the leading suit, the highest trump card (if played), or the Joker.

The Joker is the highest card of the trump suit (if trumps are played) and the only trump card at "no trumps". It can therefore be used to win a trick in a no-trump game if the player holding it is unable to follow suit.

If the Joker is played as a lead card in a no-trump game, the person playing it can name the suit that the other players must follow if possible.

The player winning a trick plays the lead card of the following trick until all ten tricks have been played.

To score
If the bidder fulfils his or her contract, he or she scores points according to the value of the contract (see below). If he or she fails to make the bid, then the player loses the equivalent number of points (and his or her score may be a minus figure).

Number of tricks

Trump suit	Six	Seven	Eight	Nine	Ten
Spades	40	140	240	340	440
Clubs	60	160	260	360	460
Diamonds	80	180	280	380	480
Hearts	100	200	300	400	500
No trump suit	120	220	320	420	520

Misère : 250
Open misère: 520

A player does not score more points than the value of the contract even if he or she won more tricks than bid. However, if a player wins all ten tricks, he or she scores 250 points, even if the value of the contract was less.

Each of the other players scores 10 points for every won trick. If the bid was misère (with the bidder aiming to lose every trick), then each non-bidder scores 10 points for every trick won by the bidder.

If no bid was made on the hand, then each player scores 10 points for every won trick.

If two players reach or exceed 500 points on the same deal, then the bidder during that deal wins the game.

Five Hundred Variations

Five Hundred can also be played by two people playing against each other, four people playing in partnerships, five playing against each other in temporary partnerships from deal to deal against the bidder, or by six people playing in two partnerships of three or three partnerships of two.

The number of cards in play usually changes as follows, with a Joker sometimes added as the top trump:

Two players 24 cards (Ace, King, Queen, Jack, ten, nine)
Three players 32 cards (Ace, King, Queen, Jack, ten, nine, eight, seven)
Four players 42 (Ace down to five plus the four of hearts and the four of diamonds)
Five players 52 cards (standard pack)
Six players 62 cards (standard pack plus elevens and twelves plus two red thirteens)

In a five-player game, the bidder can either say that he or she will play solo, or he or she can call for a partner by naming a non-trump card that he or she does *not* hold. The player holding that card then declares him- or herself and the two players play together in a partnership against the other three. (A bidder is not allowed to call for a partner if he or she bids to play misère.)

Hearts

In Hearts, the basic aim is to avoid winning any tricks containing hearts. There are many variations of the game, so before you play make sure everyone is familiar with the rules. In this section, you'll find several versions of Hearts including the most popular – Black Lady or Black Maria.

Basic Hearts

Difficulty rating
1

Number of players
3–6 (but three or four players is best)

Cards
52, with Aces ranking high.

To win
Avoid winning tricks containing hearts or score the least penalty points in a game.

To deal
The dealer deals out all the cards in the pack singly to each player, starting with the player to his or her immediate left.

If there are four players, cards can be dealt out evenly, with each player receiving 13 cards. If there are three, five or six players, it is best to remove low-ranking cards (such as the two of clubs and the two of spades) so that each player has the same number. (Note: If there are six players, four cards must be removed to get an even deal.)

To play
The player sitting on the dealer's left plays the lead card of the first trick. Each player must follow suit if possible. If a player cannot follow suit, then he or she can discard.

Players obviously try to discard any high heart cards they hold early in a game to avoid winning any tricks with hearts in them.

The winner of each trick plays the lead card of the next trick until all the cards have been played.

To score
At the end of the deal, each player adds up the number of hearts in won tricks. Each heart card counts as one point against that player. Each deal can be one game, with the player winning the most hearts losing, or scores can be kept and counted with the first player to reach an agreed total (for example, 30 points) losing the whole game.

Cancellation Hearts
In this version of hearts, two packs are shuffled together instead of one. The cards are dealt out and any remaining cards are placed face down on the table and go to the winner of the first trick (who does not need to show them to his or her opponents).

When following the lead card in a trick, if a player plays the same card (for example, the King of diamonds on the King of diamonds) then the second card cancels out the first. The trick is then won by the next-highest card, or the next-best if that is paired, and so on.

If all the cards in a trick are paired, then the trick is put on one side and goes to the winner of the trick.

Penalty points are awarded for any hearts won in tricks in the same way as for basic Hearts.

Heartsette

In Heartsette, three cards are dealt face down on the table to form a "widow". These are given to the winner of the first trick or the winner of the last trick, as agreed by the players at the beginning of the game.

Red Jack Hearts

This game is played in the same way as Hearts except that if a player wins the Jack of diamonds in a trick, then his or her total score is reduced by 10 points.

Black Lady or Black Maria

Difficulty rating
2

Number of players
3–6 (but three or four players is best)

Cards
52, with Aces ranking high.

To win
Get the lowest score by not winning tricks containing hearts or the Ace, King and Queen of spades.

To deal
The dealer deals out all the cards in the pack singly to each player, starting with the player to his or her immediate left.

As with basic Hearts, if there are four players, cards can be dealt out evenly. If there are three, five or six players, remove two, two, or four twos respectively so that the cards come out evenly.

Alternatively, any remaining cards can be placed face down on the table as a "widow", which then goes to the winner of the first trick.

To play
Before playing the first trick, each player chooses and passes three cards to the player sitting on his or her left and receives three cards from the player sitting on his or her right.

In getting rid of cards, players often try to end up with no cards in a particular suit so that they can discard any held hearts if the lead card of that suit is played in a trick.

The player sitting on the dealer's left plays the lead card of the first trick. In some versions of Black Lady, it is traditional for the player holding the two of clubs to lead with it in the first trick. (This rule obviously does not apply if the two has been removed from the pack to even up the cards for three, five or six players.)

A player who cannot follow suit can discard a high card or a penalty card (that is, a heart or the Ace, King or Queen of spades) to avoid getting the most penalty points at the end of the deal.

If a player is dealt a strong hand (such as the Ace, King, Queen and Jack of hearts and the Ace, King or Queen of spades), then he or she can opt to "shoot the moon" or win all of the heart cards and the Queen of spades.

If the player succeeds in shooting the moon, then the other players each gain 26 penalty points. If the player fails, he or she gains points according to how many hearts and penalty spades he or she has won.

A player who is trying to slam, or win all the hearts and the Queen of spades, does not have to tell the other players of his or her intention at the beginning of the deal. Once it becomes apparent as the game progresses that a player is trying to shoot the moon, then the other players must try to stop it, even if it means taking 13 penalty points by winning the Black Lady because 13 penalty points is better than 26 – the number of points given to each player if a player succeeds in a slam.

To score

Scores are totalled at the end of each deal, with penalty points being awarded as follows:

1 point – any heart

7 points – the Ace of spades

10 points – the King of spades

13 points – The Queen of spades, or the "Black Lady"

26 points – to each opponent if a player succeeds in winning all 13 hearts and the Queen of Spades

The player to reach an agreed total (such as 100 points) loses the whole game.

Klaberjass

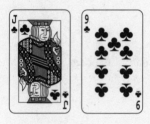

This game for two players is variously known as Clobbiosh, Clobby, Club or Kalabriasz and is very similar to the French game of Belote (see page 7). Its name is Dutch in origin and means "clover Jack" (that is, club Jack), owing to the fact that the Jack of the trump suit becomes the top trump card in the game.

Klaberjass

Difficulty rating
2

Number of players
2

Number of cards
32, with all cards below seven (except the Aces) removed from a 52-card pack.

To win
Be the first player to reach 500 points by forming scoring sequences of cards and winning tricks.

To deal
Cut the cards to decide who is going to deal first (with the highest cut winning the deal and Aces ranking low in the cut) and take it in turns to deal.

The dealer shuffles the cards then deals six cards face down to each player in two packets of three. He or she then turns the next card face up for trumps and places the rest of the pack face down to form the stock.

To bid for trumps
Before the play starts, each player takes it in turn to bid to name the trump suit, based on the cards in his or her hand. The non-dealer starts the bidding by either accepting the upcard as the trump suit, saying "Accept", passing the bidding to the dealer, saying "Pass", or proposing the cards are re-dealt, by saying "Schmeiss".

If the non-dealer passes, the dealer can either accept or pass.

Ranking of cards in Klaberjass

If the non-dealer bids "Schmeiss", then the dealer must either bid to accept trumps, agree to a new deal or pass.

If the dealer also passes, then the non-dealer gets a second turn to make a bid. If the dealer passes again, then the cards are re-dealt.

The score for each hand depends on whether or not a player chose, or made, trumps in the hand (see page 112).

Once trumps have been chosen, the dealer deals a further three cards to each player one by one, starting with his or her opponent. The card at the bottom of the pack is then turned face up on top of the pile and either player holding the seven of the trump suit, called the "dix", can exchange it for this top card.

To declare sequences

Either before the first card of the first trick is played or when the first card of the first trick is played, each player declares his or her highest held sequence by stating the number of cards in the sequence.

Declarations are made according to the points value of the sequence, which is 20 points for a three-card sequence and 50 points for a sequence of four or more cards.

The non-dealer might therefore start the declaration saying "Sequence of 20" or "Sequence of 50".

If the dealer cannot better the non-dealer's declaration, then he or she says "Good".

If the dealer can better the declaration, then he or she says "Not good". If the dealer's highest sequence is the same as that of the non-dealer, then he or she says "How high" to determine the highest-ranking card. The non-dealer then declares the rank of the highest card in the sequence and the dealer either says "Good" or "Not good" according to his or her highest card.

To score sequences
The player declaring the highest sequence must show it to his or her opponent before scoring points on it. He or she then also scores points for any other lower sequences held. The other player cannot score at this stage in the game, even if he or she holds one or more sequences of cards.

To play
The non-dealer leads with the first card of the first trick. The other player must follow suit if possible or play a trump card. If the other player cannot follow suit or play a trump, then he or she discards.

The winner of a trick leads with the first card of the following trick until all the cards have been played.

If a player holds both the King and Queen of the trump suit (called the Bella), then he or she can score 20 bonus points when playing the second of the two cards, whether or not he or she wins both tricks.

To win the points, the player must declare "Bella" when playing the first of the two cards. In some versions, the player has to declare Bella when playing the second card and always play the King before the Queen. Rules should be agreed at the beginning of the game.

The winner of the final trick in the hand scores an additional ten points.

To score tricks
Each card has a points value and points are awarded by adding up the points value of cards in each won trick.

Sequences are runs of cards of the same suit, with the cards ranking Ace, King, Queen, Jack, ten, nine, eight and seven in all four suits. If the number of cards in a sequence is equal, then the highest-ranking card in the sequence wins. If the sequences are still equal, then a sequence in the trump suit beats one in a plain suit.

20 points – for winning the trump Jack (the "jass") in a trick
14 points – for winning the trump nine (the "menel")
11 points – for every Ace
10 points – for each ten
4 points – for each King
3 points – for each Queen
2 points – for each Jack (non-trump suits)

plus

20 points – for playing and declaring the "Bella"
10 points – for winning the last trick

At the end of each hand, both players' points for sequences (one player only) and for points won in tricks are totalled and scored as follows:

• If the player choosing trumps has the most points, then each player's score stands and goes towards their final total score for the game.
• If his or her opponent has the most points, then the trump maker is said to "go bête" or "bate" and his or her opponent gets both player's points.
• If both players have the same number of points, then the player choosing trumps scores nothing (goes "half bate) and his or her opponent scores his or her own points.

The first player to reach 500 points wins the game.

Napoleon

Napoleon, or Nap, is primarily a gambling game, and a simplified version of Ecarté and Euchre. As with Ecarté and Euchre, each player in Nap is dealt five cards then bids to make a certain number of tricks.

Napoleon

Difficulty rating
2

Number of players
3–7 (but best played by 4–5)

Cards
52, with Aces ranking high. The game becomes harder by reducing the number of cards as follows:
Four players – 28 cards (removing cards below the eights excluding the Aces) or 32 cards (removing cards below seven)
Five players – 36 cards (removing cards below the sixes) or 32 cards (removing cards below five)

To win
Make a bid and win the stake.

To deal
The cards are cut to determine the first dealer then the dealer deals five cards to each player, either singly or in packets of three then two.

To bid
Starting with the player to the dealer's immediate left, each player takes a turn to bid or "pass". Each bid must be higher than the previous bid.

Players bid to win a certain number of tricks with a chosen trump suit, as follows:

"Two" – To make two tricks.

"Three" – To make three tricks.

"Miz" (short for "Misère") – To lose every trick (usually agreed with "no trumps").

"Four" – To make four tricks.

"Nap" – To make all five tricks.

"Wellington" – To make all five tricks for double stakes.

"Blücher" – To make all five tricks for redoubled stakes.

A player can only bid "Wellington" if the previous bid is "Nap" and can only bid "Blücher" after a bid of "Wellington".

To play
The highest bidder wins the contract and plays the lead card of the first trick which must be a trump card (except in "miz").

The other players must follow the suit of the lead card if possible or they can play any card. Tricks are won by the highest card of the leading suit or the highest trump if a trump is played. The winner of a trick plays the lead card of the following trick.

The play stops once the bidder has made his or her bid or is obviously going to lose it.

To score

If the bidder makes his or her bid then he or she is paid the following number of chips or counters by each opponent:

Two – 2
Three – 3
Four – 4
Miz – 3
Nap – 10
Wellington – 20
Blücher – 40

If the bidder fails to make his or her bid, then he or she has to pay the same amount to each of the other players. (By agreement, the amount paid for failing to make a bet of Nap, Wellington or Blücher may be half of the above.)

After each hand, the deal passes to the left. Usually, the cards are not shuffled between deals unless a player has made, and won, a bid of Nap.

(Also see **Ecarté** on page 86.)

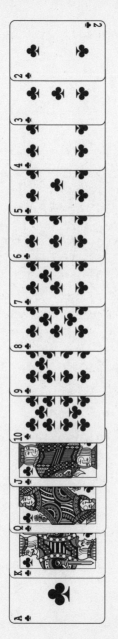

Ranking of cards in Napoleon

Piquet

Piquet is a skilled game for two players and is thought to have originated in the late 1400s or early 1500s in Britain or France. Regular Piquet players usually use two special Piquet decks of cards, keeping one shuffled and ready for the next deal while one is being used.

Piquet

Difficulty rating
3

Number of players
2

Cards
32, with all the cards below seven (except the Aces) removed from a standard 52-card pack, or a special Piquet deck of 32 cards.

High   Low

Ranking of cards in Piquet

To win
Score the most points by declaring scoring combinations of cards and taking the most tricks.

To deal
Both players cut the cards to determine the first dealer (with the player cutting the highest card dealing first). The dealer shuffles the cards, the non-dealer cuts them, then the dealer deals out 12 cards to each player (starting with his or her opponent) either in packets of two or in packets of three. (Note: Whichever method of dealing is used must remain the same throughout the whole game.)

The remaining eight cards are turned face down to form the stock and are either fanned out or divided so that the top five cards are placed sideways at a right angle to the lower three cards.

To score carte blanche

If either player has been dealt a hand containing no court cards (that is, no Kings, Queens or Jacks) then he or she immediately scores ten points for "carte blanche".

To exchange cards

Before play, each player can discard up to five cards and draw the equivalent number of cards from the stock.

The non-dealer discards first. If he or she exchanges fewer than five cards, then he or she can look at the cards (up to five) left in the stock. The dealer then has a turn to discard and can discard any number of cards depending on how many remain in the stock.

If the dealer decides not to discard, he or she may look at the cards left in the stock but must also show them to the non-dealer. If he or she does not look at the cards left in the stock, then the non-dealer cannot look at them either.

To play

In Piquet, each game is called a "partie" and consists of six deals. After exchanging cards, each player declares and scores on different combinations of cards then plays his or her cards to win tricks.

To declare combinations

There are three kinds of card combinations. Only the player with the best combination scores points for it. If both players tie in one of the card combinations, then neither player scores. The combinations are (from highest to lowest):

"Point" – Cards of the same suit (or a flush). The player with the most cards of the same suit scores one point for each of the cards held. If both players have the same number of cards in a "point", then the combined value of all the cards is taken into account and the player holding cards totalling the highest face value wins.
The face value of cards is as follows:

Aces – 11 points each

Court cards – 10 points each

Other cards – face value (that is, 10, 9 or 7 points)

"Sequence" – A run or sequence of three or more cards of the same suit, such as the ten, Jack and Queen of diamonds, or the seven, eight, nine and ten of spades.

The player holding the longest sequence scores points for *all* the sequences he or she holds, as follows (the other player scores nothing):

3 points – for three cards in a sequence, or a tierce

4 points – for four cards, or a quart

15 cards – for five cards, or a quint

16 points – for six cards, or a sectet (or sixième)

17 points – for seven cards, or a septet (or septième)

18 points – for eight cards, or an octet (or huitième)

If there is a draw, with both players holding an equal number of cards in a sequence, then the player with the highest ranking top card in the sequence wins. If both sequences are identical, then neither player scores.

"Set" – Three or four cards of the same rank, excluding nines, eights and sevens.

The player holding the most cards in a set wins the points for it as follows:

3 points – for three or more cards of the same rank (a trio)

14 points – for four or more cards of the same rank (a quatorze)

If there is a draw, with both players holding an equal number of cards in a set, then the player with the highest top ranking cards wins and scores.

To make declarations

When players declare scoring combinations of cards, each announcement is made as briefly as possible to avoid revealing too much information about the cards held. Declarations are always made in order – point, then sequence, then set.

The non-dealer begins each declaration, saying, for example "A point of four".

If the dealer cannot beat the declaration, he or she simply says "Good".

If he or she can beat the declaration, then he or she says "Not good" followed by the number of cards in his or her point.

If he or she has the same number, then he or she would say "Equal" and/or "How many?" to determine the value of the other player's "point" (that is, the combined face value of the cards).

The player who wins the point ends by saying "A point of four" (or however many cards are in the point) and "I score four" (depending on the number of cards). The score is then written down.

A sequence is declared in a similar way, with the non-dealer starting by saying, for example, "A sequence of three". The dealer would then answer saying "Good" or "Not good" depending on his or her highest held sequence.

If both players hold the same number of cards in a sequence, the dealer would ask "How high?" and the non-dealer would state the highest card in the run. The player holding the highest top card wins the point and ends by saying "A sequence of six" (or however many

cards are in the sequence) and score 16 (depending on the score value – see page 131) and write it down.

A set or meld is declared by each player stating how many cards are in his or her best meld and its rank, again starting with the non-dealer. For example, the non-dealer might say "A three of tens". The dealer would then say "Good" if he or she cannot better it or "Not good" if he or she holds a higher meld.

The winner of the declaration then states all his or her held sets and scores on all of them.

When declaring combinations of cards, a player may ask to see his or her opponent's cards to check them before they are scored.

Not every combination of cards can be claimed and scored. If a player wishes to hide the fact that he or she holds certain cards, then the player can "sink" a combination (for example, a second sequence or second set of cards) and not score on it.

Bonus points
Bonus points are also awarded as follows:

"Repique" – If one player reaches a score of 30 points for declaring and scoring on carte blanche and different combinations of cards before the other player has scored anything, then the player earns a bonus of 60 points for "repique".

"Pique" – If the non-dealer reaches 30 points on or just after leading the first card of the first trick and the dealer has not scored anything, then the non-dealer also gains a bonus of 30 points for "pique".

(Note: The dealer cannot score "pique" because the non-dealer automatically scores one point for leading the first card of the first trick.)

To play tricks

The non-dealer plays the lead card of the first trick. The other player must follow suit if possible or discard. The player winning the trick plays the lead card of the next trick and so on, until all 12 tricks have been played.

Points are awarded for tricks as follows:
1 point – for playing the lead card in a trick
1 point – for taking a trick when the lead card was played by the other player
1 point – for taking the last trick of the hand
10 points – for taking seven or more tricks
30 bonus points – for taking all 12 tricks

To score

The scores for each of the six deals in the partie, or game, are added together to give each player his or her final score. The winner is the player with the highest score.

If the other player has reached the rubicon (an agreed total of 100 points) during the partie, then the winner's score becomes 100 points plus the difference between both player's scores.

If the other player has failed to reach 100 points, then the winner's score becomes 100 points plus the combined total of both player's scores.

In some games, players play a partie of four deals rather than six. In this case, the individual scores for the first and the final deals are doubled before all the scores are added together.

Poker

Poker is a game of skill in which players use the principles of mathematics and an ability to bluff or "read" the body language of other players to win the pot, or part of the pot, on the table. Whole books have been written on playing Poker, so this section inevitably covers just the basics.

Basic Poker

Difficulty rating
3

Number of players
4–8

Cards
52, with Aces ranking high

In some games, players may agree that Aces can be used high or low (for example in low sequences or runs). Sometimes, the Joker may be added to the pack as a wild card.

To win
Stay in the game long enough to win the pot by bluffing or holding the best hand.

To deal
The dealer can be chosen by cutting the cards (with the player drawing the highest or lowest card, by agreement, dealing first) or by someone dealing out the cards face up, one at a time, until one player gets a Jack. That player then becomes the first dealer.

Players can either sit where they please around the table or the cards can be cut to decide where each player sits, with the player drawing the lowest card sitting to the immediate left of the dealer, the player drawing the next-lowest sitting to the left of that player, and so on. If two players draw a card of the same rank, then they draw again.

The dealer shuffles the cards and offers the pack to the player on his or her left to cut them. The player can either cut them or refuse. If the player refuses, then the dealer offers the pack to the next player to cut the cards, and so on.

If all the players refuse to the cut the cards, the dealer deals out five cards to each player, starting with the player to his or left. The cards are usually dealt in two packets of two, face down, then a single card face up.

To run the pot
In most games, one player becomes the banker and looks after the counters, or chips, and the pot. Before the first deal, each player puts up, or antes, a number of chips into the pot.

The amount of the ante should be decided at the beginning of the game, as well as how much each bet should be, how many times a bet can be raised and a timeframe for the game.

Poker hands
Poker hands are as follows, starting with the highest:

• **Royal straight flush** – A sequence of five cards of the same suit running Ace, King, Queen, Jack and ten. This hand is unbeatable if the Joker isn't being played. If the Joker is being played then theoretically five of a kind – four cards of the same rank combined with the Joker – is the highest-possible hand.

• **Straight flush** – A sequence or run of five cards of the same suit ranked by the highest card in the run, so a run with a nine as its highest card would be termed a "straight flush nine high".

• **Four of a kind** – Four cards of the same rank. If tied, then higher ranking cards beat lower ranking cards. For example, four Jacks beat four tens.

• **Full house** – Three of a kind (three cards of the same rank) and a pair, such as three Queens and two eights. If tied, the triplet determines the winner, so three Queens and two eights beats three Jacks and two tens.

• **Flush** – Five cards of the same suit but not in a sequence. If tied, the highest card in the flush wins. If still tied, then the second-highest card wins, and so on.

• **Straight** – A sequence or run of five cards of different suits. Aces can count high or low, so runs of Ace, King, Queen, Jack, ten or of Ace, two, three, four, five are allowed.

• **Three of a kind** – Three cards of the same rank with the other two cards unmatched. If tied, the highest-ranking triplet wins.

• **Two pairs** – (with one unmatched card). If tied, the hand holding the highest pair wins. For example a pair of tens and fours beats a pair of nines and sevens.

• **One pair** – (with three unmatched cards) If tied, the hand with the highest pair wins.

• **High card** – No card combination but with one card simply being the highest held in the hand. If tied, the hand with the second-highest card wins.

• **Five of a kind** – Five cards of the same rank, which is only possible if the Joker is being played as a wild card (or any other cards are given the status of wild card).

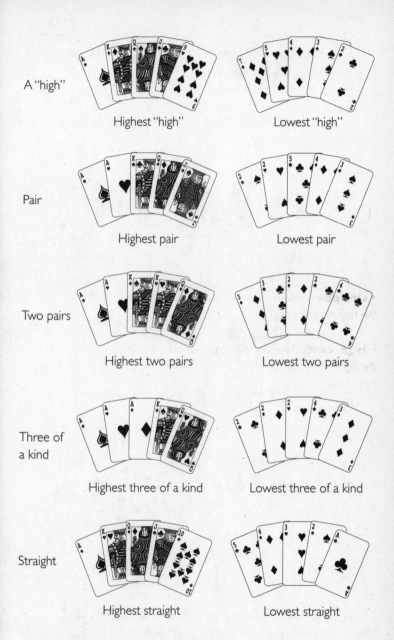

A "high"

Highest "high"   Lowest "high"

Pair

Highest pair   Lowest pair

Two pairs

Highest two pairs   Lowest two pairs

Three of
a kind

Highest three of a kind   Lowest three of a kind

Straight

Highest straight   Lowest straight

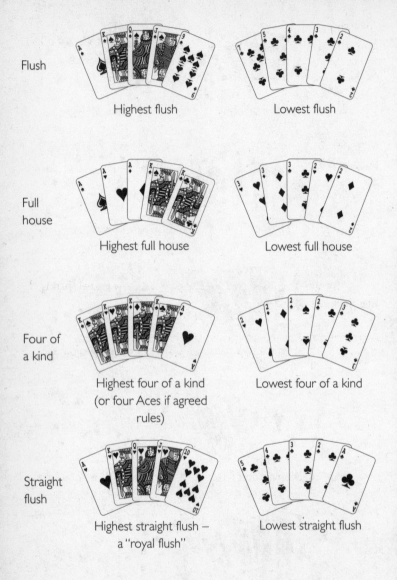

Flush	Highest flush	Lowest flush
Full house	Highest full house	Lowest full house
Four of a kind	Highest four of a kind (or four Aces if agreed rules)	Lowest four of a kind
Straight flush	Highest straight flush – a "royal flush"	Lowest straight flush

A higher poker hand beats a lower poker hand, with a hand holding a straight flush being the highest and a "high" the lowest.

To play

Each player looks at his or her hand and then one player makes the opening bet (or "opens the pot"). Rules vary according to which player opens the pot first and the minimum (and maximum) bet.

Before the pot is open, each player in turn can do one of the following:
- Make a bet (or "check"), with the first player to do so therefore opening the pot
- Pass (or "check")
- Fold or drop out by laying his or her cards face down on the table.

A player who folds can take no further part in the hand and has no claim on the pot.

If no player opens the pot, then all the players throw in their hands and there is a new deal.

Once the pot is open, each player who has not folded can:
- Match, by increasing his or her stake in the pot to match that put in by the previous player.
- Raise, by matching the stake of the previous player and increasing it further.
- Call, by matching the previous player's raised stake and call an ending to the bidding.
- Fold, by throwing in his or her cards.

Once a player has been called, he or she cannot raise the stakes again and the betting is over. In some games of Poker, this may be followed by a showdown in which each player reveals his or her hand and the best hand wins the pot, with the cards speaking for themselves.

If a player raises and none of the other players call but throw in their cards, then the player wins the pot without having to show his or her cards to the other players.

Draw Poker

Difficulty rating
3

Number of players
4–6 (but best played with five players)

Cards
52, with Aces ranking high

To win
Stay in the game long enough to win the pot by bluffing or holding the best hand.

To deal
The seating arrangements and dealer are chosen by an agreed method (see Basic Poker, page 134) and each player takes a turn to deal. The dealer shuffles the cards well then deals out five cards to each player, one at a time and face down.

To play
Each player, starting with the player to the immediate left of the dealer, can either make an opening bet, pass or fold until the pot is open.

If all the players pass, then the cards are thrown in and redealt and the pot is carried forward to the next deal.

Once a player has opened the pot, each player can match the previous player's bet and call, raise the stakes, or fold.

If one player raises the stakes and the remaining players fold, then that player wins the pot.

If one player calls another then there is a draw. In the draw, each player (starting with the player to the immediate left of the dealer) either stands or calls to exchange cards. To exchange cards, a player puts one, two or three cards from his or her hand face down on the table and announces how many cards he or she wants drawn from the pack.

Each player then looks at his or her cards and there is a second round of betting.

The player who opened the pot on the first round starts the second and each player in turn can pass or check (often by knocking on the table) or bet. If every player passes, then the player who opened the first pot must open it for the second time.

Once the pot has been opened for the second round, each player in turn can either call by matching the previous player's stake, raise or fold.

Play continues in this way until there is a showdown and the player holding the best hand wins the pot.

Draw Poker Variations

There are several variations of Draw Poker. Here are some of the most common.

Deuces Wild

Each deuce, or two, ranks as a wild card and can be used in place of any other card except to replace a card already held. The highest hand that beats any other, by agreement, then becomes five of a kind. Some players, however, prefer a royal flush to still be the unbeatable hand. If hands are tied, then the hand containing most natural (non-wild) cards wins.

Lowball

In Lowball, the lowest-ranking hand rather than the highest wins the pot. Straights and flushes do not count and Aces are always low, so a pair of Aces is lower than a pair of twos and the lowest possible hand is Ace, two, three, four, five, known as a "wheel" or "bicycle".

In Lowball, there is usually no minimum stake to open the pot and players can check or pass during play. If none of the players bet (after the dealer has called for bets twice), then there is a showdown. The players left in the round show their cards and the player holding the lowest hand wins the pot.

Hi-Lo Draw

In this type of Draw Poker, the pot is split evenly between the two players holding the highest and the lowest hands. The lowest hand is one containing a "high" so the lowest possible hand is a seven, five, four, three and two of different suits or a six, four, three, two and Ace if Aces are counted low. (The latter hand is also known as a Sixty-Four.)

Stud Poker

Five-Card Stud

Difficulty rating
3

Number of players
4–8

Cards
52, with Aces ranking high

To win
Stay in the game long enough to win the pot by bluffing or holding the best hand.

To deal
Before dealing, the dealer antes one counter, or chip, for each player in the game. He or she then deals each player one card face down (called the "hold" card) and one card face up.

After a round of betting (see below), the dealer deals out a second card face up. There is a further round of betting, then the dealer deals out a third card then a fourth card, again face up, with another round of betting in between.

To play
After the dealer has dealt out the first two cards, the player holding the highest face up card or (if there is a tie), the player sitting nearest the dealer's left, starts the play.

Each player in turn either makes a bet or throws in his or her cards. When the first round of betting is completed and all bets are equalized, the dealer deals out another face-up card to each player. After each deal, the player holding the best combination of face-up cards is the first to bet. If that player drops out of the deal, then the player holding the next-best combination starts, and so on until each player has been dealt five cards in total.

Once all players pass during the final (fourth) round of betting, there is a showdown. Each player reveals his or her "hole card" and the player with the best poker hand wins the pot.

Seven-Card Stud

In Seven-Card Stud, the dealer deals two cards face down and one card face up in the first deal. Each player then bets as described in Five-Card Stud. After the first round of betting, the dealer then deals out a further three cards to each player one at a time and face up, with each deal being followed by a round of betting. The seventh and final card of the hand is dealt face down. Each player looks at his or her cards and there is a final round of betting followed by the show-down in which each player selects his or her best five cards to make up a Poker hand. The best hand wins the pot.

If two hands are identical, the discarded cards are used to determine the winner.

Pontoon

Pontoon (also known as Blackjack in the United States and "Vingt-et-Un" (Twenty-one) in France) is a well-known gambling game. A "pontoon" is combination of an Ace with a ten or a court card, whose total face value is 21.

Pontoon

Difficulty rating

I

Number of players

2–8 or more (but best played with 5–8)

Cards

52 (with two packs for eight or more players). Aces can count as eleven points or one point, court cards count ten points each and other cards count as their face value.

To win

Have a hand in which the total face value of the cards adds up to 21 or which is higher than that of the banker, or dealer.

To deal

The cards are usually cut to determine the banker, with the player cutting the highest card dealing first.

The banker deals one card to each player, starting with the player to his or her left and ending with him or herself. Each player (except the banker) looks at his or her cards and places several chips or counters on the table as a stake.

The banker does not need to bet on the cards. If the banker does make a bet, then he or she must stake twice the amount of the highest bet on the table.

The banker then deals a second card to each player but still does not look at his or her own cards.

If any player has a "pontoon" (a 21 consisting of an Ace and a court card or an Ace and a ten), he or she turns the Ace face up on top of the other card and stakes nothing more.

If a player has two cards of the same rank (for example, two tens or two Jacks), then he or she can split them by laying them face up on the table and placing another stake that is equal to his or her first stake. The banker then deals another card face down on each of the cards. If these cards also happen to be the same rank, then the cards can be split again. When it is the player's turn to play, he or she can play each of the hands in turn.

To play
The banker asks each player in turn whether he or she wants more cards. The player may then do one of the following:

"Stick" – If the player has a count of at least 15 (to be agreed), he or she may stick and not take any more cards.
"Buy" – If the player wishes, he or she can increase his or her stake and buy another card (saying "Buy one"). The card is then dealt face down. The stake cannot be less than the player's previous stake and cannot be more than double it. If the player wants another card, he or she can buy it or "twist" – see below.
"Twist" – If the player likes, he or she can receive more cards from the banker (up to a maximum of five) without raising his or her initial stake by saying "twist". In this case, the banker deals the player a card face up on the table. Five cards totalling less than 21 make up a Five-Card Trick. Once a player has twisted, he or she cannot then increase his or her stake by buying another card.

Each player buys or twists until he or she either sticks or goes "bust" – when the total face value of cards exceeds 21. If a player goes bust, he or she must pay his stake to the banker and throw in his or her cards face up, which are then placed at the bottom of the pack.

If a player has a split hand and goes bust on the first one, he or she can still play the other hand.

Once the banker has gone round all the players he or she turns up his or her cards and turns up more cards until he or she sticks or busts.

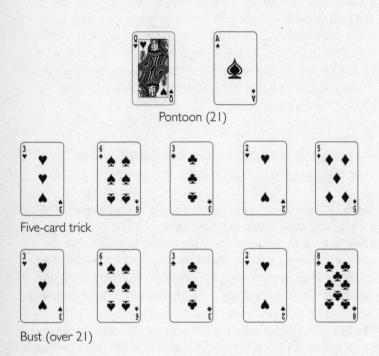

Pontoon (21)

Five-card trick

Bust (over 21)

To pay out

• If the dealer gets a Five-Card Trick, he or she only pays a player with a Pontoon at double his or her stake.

• If the dealer gets a pontoon, he or she wins all the other players' stakes (even if another player also has a pontoon).

• If the dealer gets 21 with three or more cards, he or she must pay double stakes to any player with a pontoon or a Five-Card Trick but wins all the other players' stakes.

• If the dealer gets less than 21, he or she pays back any player with a higher card count their stake but collects from those players with an equal or lower card count. For example, if the dealer sticks at 18, then he or she pays any opponent whose cards add up to 19, 20 or 21.

• If the dealer goes bust, he or she pays anyone with a count of 16 or more but keeps the stakes of any player who also went bust.

• If the dealer doubled the initial highest bet earlier in the game, the banker's winnings or payouts are doubled.

The cards are not usually shuffled after each deal unless a player gets a pontoon. That player then usually becomes the banker. A banker can also sell the bank to any of the other players after a round.

Rummy

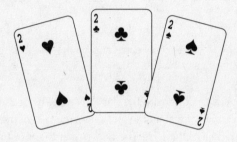

Rummy is a well-known card game with several variations, one of the most popular being Gin Rummy. Canasta, another rummy game, was developed in South America in the mid-1940s and soon spread to America and Britain...

Basic Rummy

Difficulty rating
1

Number of players
2–8

Cards
52 (two packs if there are six or more players), with Aces ranking low

To win
Collect sets or combinations of cards and be the first to discard them

To deal
The cards are cut to determine the dealer. The dealer deals out seven cards to each player one at a time and stacks the rest of the pack face down in the middle of the table. The deal passes to the left around the table and each dealer must shuffle the cards well between each hand.

The number of cards dealt varies according to the number of players, as follows:
2 players – 10 cards each
3–4 players – 7 cards each
5–6 players – 6 cards each

To play
The player to the immediate left of the dealer is the first to play. He or she takes the top card from the stock, adds it to his or her hand, then discards one card face up next to the pile of stock to start the discard pile.

The next player either takes the top card of the discard pile (called the upcard) or a face-down card from the stock, adds it to his or her hand, then discards a card. Play continues around the table, with each player taking a card and discarding to form sets or combinations of cards, called "melds".

Sets are three or more cards of the same rank (such as three Jacks or three sixes and so on). Melds are sequences of three or more cards of the same suit (such as six-seven-eight of hearts, or ten-Jack-Queen of spades).

Set   Sequence

Examples of melds in basic Rummy. When melding cards, Aces count as low and Kings high, so a sequence running Queen-King-Ace is not allowed.

Once a player has formed a meld of three or four cards, he or she can lay it down on the table face up. (A newly formed meld should be placed on the table before discarding.) Some players, however, prefer to keep melds in their hands for as long as possible.

Once cards have been placed on the table in a meld, the cards in the set or sequence cannot be moved to another meld.

When a player has formed at least one meld, he or she can discard single cards left in his or her hand by adding them to any melds laid on the table. For example, he or she can place a fourth six on three sixes, or a Jack of spades on a sequence running eight-nine-ten of spades.

If a player manages to place all the cards in his or her hand on the table in one go (without laying down earlier melds or laying off single cards), he or she is said to "go rummy".

The hand ends as soon as one player has played his or her last card.

The cards left in the other players' hands are then scored and awarded to the winner, as follows:
Ace – I point
Other cards – face value (that is, 2–10 points each)
Court cards – 10 points each
(In some variations, court cards are scored separately, with the Jack being 11 points, the Queen 12 points and the King 13 points.)
Because court cards earn their holders the most penalty points, it is obviously advantageous to discard these early on in the game.

The winner is the first player to reach an agreed number of points after as many deals as necessary.

Gin Rummy

Difficulty rating
1

Number of players
2

Cards
52, with Aces ranking low

To win
Be the first to meld cards in sets or sequences

To deal
The cards are cut to determine the first dealer. The dealer shuffles the cards well then deals out ten cards one by one starting with his or her opponent. The dealer then turns up the next card to start the discard pile and places it on the table alongside the rest of the pack, which remains face down to form the stock.

To play
The non-dealer starts by either taking the upcard or refusing it. If he or she does not take it, then the dealer can either take it or refuse it. If neither player takes the upcard, then the non-dealer takes the top card from the pile of stock and discards a card face up on the discard pile.

As with basic Rummy, each player aims to build sets of three or four cards of the same rank or a sequence of three or four cards of the same suit (see page 154) and be the first to "go gin" (by laying out all the cards in the hand on the table in one go) or "knock" (see overleaf).

To knock

A player has the option of knocking when the combined total of the unmelded, single cards in the hand (called the "deadwood") is ten points or less.

To do this, the player simply knocks on the table after drawing and discarding, then sets out all his or her cards. The other player then sets out his or her hand, too, and (if possible), lays off any deadwood to his or her opponent's melds. (He or she can only do this if the player going out has not gone gin.)

To score

A player going gin scores 20 points (sometimes agreed at 10 or 25 points).

A player who knocked who has less deadwood (that is, fewer card-points) than his or her opponent scores the difference between each deadwood. However, if the knocker's opponent has less deadwood, then the opponent scores the difference between each deadwood plus an extra 20 points (sometimes agreed at 10 or 25 points).

Each player takes it in turn to deal and a running score is kept on paper. The winner is the first player to reach 100 points.

Gin Rummy Variations

There are several variations of Gin Rummy. Here are two of them.

Oklahoma Gin Rummy

This is played in exactly the same way as Gin Rummy except that the upcard (the first card turned up from the stock) decides the maximum number at which a player may go knocking. For example, if the turn-up is a six, then a player can only knock when he or she has six or fewer deadwood (combined total of card-points) in his or her hand.

Around the Corner Gin Rummy

In this variation of Gin Rummy, card sequences can go "around the corner" so a sequence running King, Ace, two or one running Ace, King, Queen is allowed. Scoring is the same except that an unmelded Ace is usually 15 points. In addition, the player who does not knock is allowed to lay off any single cards onto his or her opponent's melds even if that opponent has gone "gin".

500 Rummy

Difficulty rating

1

Number of players

3–8

Cards

52 (or two packs when there are 5–8 players)

To win

Be the first player to score 500 points.

To deal

The cards are cut to determine the first dealer. The dealer deals seven cards to each player, one by one. As with basic Rummy, the deal passes to the left each time and the dealer shuffles the pack well between hands.

To play

The game is played in the same way as basic Rummy with every player either drawing the top card from the pile or stock or the top card from the discard pile. In addition, however, a player can also draw any card from the discard pile as long as he or she immediately forms a meld with it. A player can also pick up all the cards in the discard pile that lie above the selected card and use them to make as many melds as desired. In order to view all the cards in the discard pile, the cards are not stacked but are spread out in a fan without mixing up their order. A player's turn ends when he or she discards a card.

Players form melds by grouping cards of the same rank or cards of the same suit running in a sequence. Each player can add cards to his or her own melds or to those laid down by another player, as in basic Rummy.

If all the stockpile is used up before any player melds all his or her cards, each player takes turns drawing a card from the discard pile.

As soon as a player gets rid of all his or her cards, either by making a meld using all the cards in his or her hand or by making a meld and discarding a final card, the play ends.

To score

Each player adds up the value of the cards he or she has melded and the unmelded cards left in his or her hand. Each player's score is the difference between the two figures.

Card values are as follows:
Ace – 1 point or 15 points (depending on whether or not it has been melded in a low or a high sequence of cards)
Court cards – 10 points each
Other cards – face value

Scores are kept on paper and the first player to reach 500 points wins the game.

Kaluki

Difficulty rating
2

Number of players
2–6 (but best played with four)

Cards
Two packs plus Jokers

To win
Have the lowest penalty points when another player loses the game.

To deal
The cards are cut to determine the first dealer. The dealer shuffles both packs of cards including the two Jokers and deals one card to each player, singly and face down, as follows:

15 cards each if there are four players
13 cards each if there are five players
11 cards each if there are six players

The dealer turns the next card face up and places it in the middle of the table. The rest of the cards are placed face down alongside to form the stock.

To play
The player to the immediate left of the dealer begins by picking up a card from the stock then discarding a card. Play continues with each player taking a turn to pick up and discard, all the time aiming to form and lay down melds. As soon as each player forms a meld, it is placed face-up on the table.

Each player must take a card from the stock until he or she has made at least one meld. A player can only take the upcard (the top card of the discard pile) before he or she has made a meld if the upcard can be used in that player's first meld, which must be placed immediately on the table. Once a player has made a meld, he or she can lay off single cards if desired onto either end of another player's displayed melds.

Melds, or sets, can be three or four cards of the same rank, or three or four cards of the same suit in a consecutive sequence. In forming sets of the same rank, each card in the set must be of a different suit, so holding two Aces of hearts or two Aces of spades for example is not allowed. In forming sequences, an Ace can be part of a run with a King, Queen and Jack or it can be part of a run of Ace, two, three. It cannot be used in a meld running King, Ace, two.

Jokers can be used to represent any other card.

The first meld that any player lays down on the table must have a total value of 40 points or more (or 51 points in some versions of the game). The meld can be worth less as long as the player lays off single cards from his or her hand onto other players' melds at the same time and the total value of the meld and the laid-off cards is at least 40 (51) points.

For the purposes of scoring, each card has the following values:
Jokers – 15 points each
Aces – 11 points each
Court cards – 10 points each
Other cards – face value

Once a player has formed an opening meld, he or she has several options when it is his or her turn to play. The player can:
• form a new meld of three or four cards
• place a card at either end of another player's sequence
• take a Joker from another player's meld when it is in the middle of a sequence and swap it with the actual card it represents from his or her hand. However, the player can only do this if he or she immediately lays the Joker on the table as part of a new set or plays it at the end of an existing run.
• take a Joker from another player's meld when it is part of a set of three cards of the same rank and replace it with the two missing actual cards that make up the set. For example, if the set is three of clubs, three of spades and a Joker, a player could add the three of hearts and the three of diamonds if held as long as he or she can meld the Joker in a new set. Alternatively, the player can remove the Joker, add just one of the missing threes that makes up a set and declare the set closed. Once a set has been declared closed, another player cannot add to it or remove the Joker, as described.

A player who is down to his or her last three, then two, then one card must announce this to the rest of the players.

The hand ends as soon as one player has played his or her last card.

If a player manages to place all the cards in his or her hand on the table in one go (without laying down earlier melds or laying off single cards), he or she is said to "go Kaluki".

The cards left in the other players' hands when one player has gone out are then scored (see page 163). The first player to reach an agreed number of penalty points (usually 150) loses the game.

In some versions, players have three lives. The first time a player loses a game (by being the first to reach 150 penalty points) he or she loses one life. The player starts the next game carrying penalty points, which equal the penalty points of the player with the second-highest penalty score. Once a player loses three lives, he or she is out of the game.

Canasta

Difficulty rating
2

Number of players
2–4 (but mostly played by four players playing in partnerships)

Cards
Two packs plus four Jokers

To win
Be the first partnership to reach an agreed number of points over as many deals as necessary.

To deal

The cards are cut to determine the partnerships and the first dealer. The dealer shuffles both packs of cards well then deals out eleven cards to each player, one by one, starting with the player to his or her immediate left. The rest of the cards are placed in the middle of the table to form the stock and the top card of the stock is turned face-up and placed alongside to start the discard pile, or wastepile. If this upcard is a Joker, a two, or a red three, then the dealer must turn up the next card from the stockpile and place it on top. He or she must repeat this if the next card is also a Joker, a two or a red three, until the upcard is of a different rank.

To make melds

Each player aims to make melds of three or more cards of the same rank (except Jokers, twos and threes).

Each of the Jokers and twos are "wild cards" and can be used to make up a meld with any other rank of card except threes. However, every meld must contain at least two "non-wild" cards and no more than three wild cards.

Red threes are bonus cards and each is worth 100 points. Black threes cannot be melded but can be used to "freeze" or "stop" the discard pile so the next player cannot use any of the cards in it (see overleaf).

A "canasta" is a meld of seven or eight cards of the same rank and must contain at least four non-wild, or natural, cards.

To play

The player to the immediate left of the dealer starts the game and the play passes to the left around the table.

If any player holds a red three, then he or she must lay it face up on the table before his or her first turn. Similarly, if a player draws a red three from the stock, it is placed face up on the table alongside any meld, or melds, and the player draws a fresh card from the stock to replace it.

Each player takes it in turn to draw a card, meld a set of cards if desired, then discard a card.

The first meld made by either player in a partnership must be made up of cards whose combined value reaches a certain figure, depending on the partnership's current score:

Current score of partnership:	Meld must be worth at least:
0–1500	50 points
1500–3000	90 points
3000 or more	120 points

(A partnership's opening meld must therefore be worth at least 50 points.)

For scoring, each card has the following values:

Red threes	100 points each
Jokers	50 points each
Aces	20 points each
Twos	20 points each
Kings, Queens, Jacks, tens, nines, eights	10 points each
Sevens, sixes, fives, fours	5 points each
Black threes	5 points each

When drawing a card, a player can either draw the top card from the stock or take the top card of the discard pile. A player also has the option of taking the whole of the discard pile if he or she has two cards of the same rank as the upturned card. If a player does this, then he or she must be able to use the upcard immediately in a meld and lay it on the table. The player can then lay down further melds using cards in his or her hand and cards in the discard pile before discarding a card (and starting a new discard pile).

Capturing the discard pile gives players more opportunities of forming melds, so players are also able to prevent the next player from capturing it by "stopping" or "freezing" it.

Stopping – If a player discards a black three, this stops the next player from capturing the discard pile. The following player, however, can capture the discard pile when it is his or her turn by laying down a meld using the black three on top of the pile.

Freezing – If a player places a wild card (a Joker or a two) at right angles across the top of the discard pile, this freezes the cards below and means that they cannot be captured until a meld is made using the next upcard on the pile combined with two natural cards of the same rank. The player who makes this meld can unfreeze the cards and capture them all. A player who is unable to unfreeze the pack must take the top card from the stock. He or she can then form a new meld or lay off a card to an existing meld but cannot capture the discard pile on that turn.

Once a player has formed a meld, either that player or his or her partner can add to it when it is his or her turn to play. Cards added to a meld can either be of the same rank or one or more wild cards. A player can only lay off cards onto his or her own melds or those of his or her partner, and wild cards cannot be moved from one displayed meld to another.

When a meld becomes a canasta (seven cards), it is arranged in a pile with:
• a red card on top if it only contains natural, or non-wild cards
• a black card on top if it contains any wild cards

If a wild card is later laid off onto a red canasta (that is, by a player adding an eighth card to a canasta of seven), then the top card must be changed from red to black.

Each player must keep at least two cards in his or her hand until ready to "meld out" (see below).

To meld out

A player "melds out" when he or she plays the last card from his or her hand (either by laying it onto a meld or by discarding it). To meld out, the player's partnership must have already formed one canasta and the player must have asked (and received) his or her partner's agreement.

A player who holds one black three can meld out simply by discarding it. If the player holds three or four black threes, then they can be melded together and the player can go out. However, if the player holds just two black threes, he or she cannot meld out.

If the pile of stock is used up before anyone melds all of his or her cards, then play continues without a stockpile with each player taking the upcard if he or she can form a meld with it or lay it off on one of his or her partner's melds. The play continues in this way until a player melds out or any player cannot use the previous player's discard.

To score

Each partnership scores the combined value of all melded cards plus:

500 points – for every canasta without wild cards (red card on top)

300 points – for every canasta containing wild cards (black card on top)

100 points – for making the last meld ("melding out")

200 points – for melding out concealed (that is, melding all cards at the same time, without having laid any off or made any earlier melds)

100 points – for every declared red three

200 points –   for the partnership holding all four
                red threes

The combined value of all unmelded cards is then
deducted from this score.

If the partnership did not make a single meld, then 100
points per red three held is also deducted from the
partnership's total score
(or 800 if the partnership held all four red threes).

Points are also deducted as follows:
500 points – for holding a red three that has not been declared
100 points – for melding out without partner's permission
100 points – for being unable to meld out after gaining partner's
                permission
50 points –   for taking an upcard without being able to use it in a
                meld

Running totals are kept on a scoresheet and the first partnership to
reach an agreed total score (usually 5000) wins the game.

Canasta Variations
Canasta can be played by two players with the same rules as above
except that the dealer deals out 15 cards each. If there are three
players, each player is dealt 13 cards and plays solo.

Seven-Up

Seven-up (formerly known as All Fours in Britain) is a good game for 2–4 players. Variations include California Jack and Auction Pitch. Auction Pitch is especially popular in the United States.

Seven-Up

Difficulty rating
2

Number of players
2–3 (can also be played by four people in partnerships)

Cards
52, with Aces counting high

To win
Score seven (or sometimes ten) points, as agreed at the beginning of the game.

To deal
Cut the cards to decide who is going to deal. The person with the highest cut becomes the first dealer.

The dealer deals six cards to each player, three at a time, from left to right. He or she then turns up the next card to show the "trump" suit. If the dealer turns up a Jack, then he or she immediately scores one point. Players take it in turns to deal, moving clockwise around the table.

To pick trumps
If there are only two people playing, both players look at their hands. If three or more players are playing, then only the dealer and the player to his or her immediate left look at their hands.

If the player to the dealer's left is happy with the trump suit then he or she calls "I stand" or "Stand" and plays the first card of the game. If the player is not happy with the trump suit, then he or she calls "I beg" or "Beg" and the dealer then chooses to keep the trump suit or change it.

If the dealer doesn't want to change the trump suit, he or she gives the other player one point. (The only time the dealer cannot do this is if the extra point would mean the other player wins the whole game.)

If the dealer decides to change the trump suit, he or she deals each player another three cards, three at a time, and turns up the next card to decide the trump suit. If it is the same suit as the first trump card, then the dealer deals out a further three cards to each player and turns up the following card. If that card is still not a different trump suit, then the dealer carries on dealing cards three at a time and turning up the next card until a different trump suit comes up. This is called running the deck. The dealer does *not* score one point for a Jack when it is turned up while running the deck: he or she only scores for a Jack if it is the first trump turned up at the beginning of the deal.

If a new trump card is turned up while the dealer is running the deck, then each player picks his or her best six cards and discards the others. If no new trump suit is turned up while running the deck, then the dealer collects all the cards and redeals them.

To play
The player immediately to the dealer's left leads with the first card of the first trick. If the card played is a trump card, then each player must also play a trump card if possible. If the card played is not a trump card, then each player must try to play a card of the same suit. If a player cannot follow suit, he or she can either play a trump card and win the trick, or play a card of a different suit.

The highest card in the trick wins the trick unless a trump card has been played. Then, the highest trump wins the trick.

Play continues until all six tricks have been won. Each player puts tricks he or she has won face down on the table. Tricks are turned face up at the end of the hand for scoring.

To score

1 point is given for a High – for the highest trump in a won trick

1 point is given for a Low – for the lowest trump in a won trick

1 point is given for a Jack – for the Jack of the trump suit taken in a trick, or to the dealer who turns up a Jack as the first trump card at the beginning of a game

1 point is given for "game" – to the player with the highest number of points taken in won tricks. Points are awarded as follows:

10 – 10 points
Ace – 4 points
King – 3 points
Queen – 2 points
Jack – 1 point

If there is a tie in the number of points between the dealer and the other player, then the dealer wins the hand. If three or more players are playing and there is a tie between two players excluding the dealer, then no one scores a point for "game".

If a player holds the only trump card, then he or she will win a point for both High and Low. If that card happens to be a trump Jack, then the player would win three points for High, Low and Jack.

Each hand is won by the player scoring the highest number of points. Further hands are played until one player scores seven (or sometimes ten) points. That player then wins the whole game.

In the hand of Seven-Up (illustrated opposite), the first trump suit is hearts. The non-dealer begs and the dealer also rejects hearts as trumps. The dealer then deals out a further three cards. As another heart is turned up as trumps, the dealer must run the deck again. Both players now accept spades as trumps and discard their weakest cards. In this game, the non-dealer would win points for High, Low, Jack and "game".

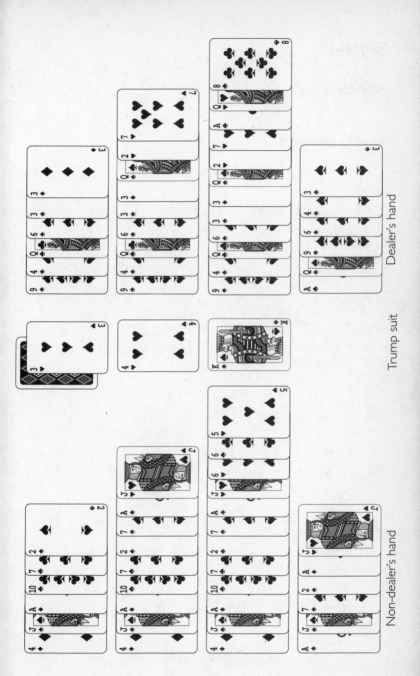

Trump suit

Dealer's hand

Non-dealer's hand

— 175 —

All Fives

Difficulty rating
2

Number of players
2

Cards
52, with Aces counting high

To win
Score 61 points.

To play
This is a variation of Seven-Up for two players. The play is the same as for Seven-Up, with the same scoring for High, Low, Jack and "game". In addition, players score extra points if they win any of the following trumps in a trick:

5 – 5 points
10 – 10 points
Ace – 4 points
King – 3 points
Queen – 2 points
Jack – 1 point

The first player to get 61 points wins. Usually, a cribbage board is used to keep count (see page 77).

Auction Pitch

Difficulty rating
2

Number of players
2–7 (with playing in a partnership optional)

Cards
52, with Aces counting high

To win
Either to win each game according to whether or not a bid is successful (see page 178) or to score seven (or sometimes more) points.

To deal
The dealer deals six cards to each player, three at a time, from left to right, as for Seven-Up. However, the dealer does not turn up the next card to find out the trump suit. Instead, each player makes a bid to name the trump suit.

To bid for trumps
Each player makes a bid according to the number of points (High, Low, Jack and "game") that the player thinks he or she can win in the hand, with a maximum number of four.

The player sitting to the immediate left of the dealer starts the bidding. If he or she bids four points, then the game starts, and that player leads with a trump card. If the player accidentally (or intentionally) pitches a wrong card (that is, not a declared trump), then the suit of the pitched card becomes trumps instead.

If the player does not want to bid he or she says "Pass" and the bid passes to the player on his or her immediate left, who can then bet from one to four points. Each player in turn may either pass or bid at least one point more than the previous bid until each player has had a chance to make a bid. The highest bidder starts the play.

To play

Play is the same as for Seven-Up. Once the first card has been played, players must follow suit or play a trump card. The trick is taken by the highest card of the lead suit or the highest trump if a trump is played.

To score

In a simplified game, the bidder wins the hand, or game, if he or she wins the same number of points bid at the start.

In a scoring game, the winner is the first to reach 7, 10 or 11 points (the target number of points being agreed at the beginning of the game). Points are given for High, Low, Jack and "game", as in Seven-Up. However, there is no point for Jack if the trump Jack is not dealt during the game. There is also no point for "game" if two or more people reach the same number of points during a hand.

If the bidder does not win the stated number of tricks, then he or she must deduct that number from his or her score. If that player's score becomes less than zero, the player is "in the hole" and his or her score is either circled or written with a minus sign in front of it.

If two or more people including the bidder or pitcher reach the target number of points to win the whole game (that is, 7, 10 or 11) in the same hand, then the person who was the bidder in that final hand wins.

Auction Pitch Variations

Here are two variations of Auction Pitch. If you decide to play one of them, make sure all the players are clear about the rules.

1. The dealer may become the pitcher by matching the highest bid made or, if each player passes instead of bids, by bidding at least one.

2. Any player who is in the hole may "smudge" by bidding four points. If he or she is successful in winning that number of points in the following hand, he or she wins the whole game.

California Jack

Difficulty rating
2

Number of players
2

Cards
52, with Aces counting high

To win
Score 7 points (or another agreed number)

To deal
The dealer deals six cards in packets of threes then turns up the next card for trumps, as for Seven-Up. The trump card is then buried in the rest of the pack of undealt cards and the cards are placed face up in a pile in the middle of the table.

To play

The non-dealer leads. The game is played in the same way as Seven-Up with each player following suit if possible to win each trick. If a player cannot follow suit, then he or she can play any card. In this variation of Seven-Up, however, players cannot play a trump card to win a trick if they are able to follow suit. Each trick is taken by the highest card of each suit or by the highest trump card, if played.

The winner of each trick takes another card from the stock, followed by the other player. The winner of a trick plays the lead card of the next trick.

To score

As for Seven-Up:

1 point is given for a High – for the highest trump in a won trick

1 point is given for a Low – for the lowest trump in a won trick

1 point is given for a Jack – for the Jack of the trump suit taken in a trick, or to the dealer who turns up a Jack as the first trump card at the beginning of a game

1 point is given for "game" – here, "game" is 41 or more points

Points are awarded in the same way as for Seven-Up:

10 – 10 points
Ace – 4 points
King – 3 points
Queen – 2 points
Jack – 1 point

The whole game is won by the first player reaching a total of 7 (or another agreed number). California Jack can also be played with the same scoring system as for All Fives, with extra points scored for trumps won in tricks (see page 176).

Shasta Sam

This game is played exactly the same as California Jack except that the stock of cards is placed face down on the table rather than face up.

Skat

Skat was developed in Germany in the 19th century and became popular in many European countries and the United States, with slight variations. It is a good card game for three players.

Skat

Difficulty rating
3

Number of players
3 (although 4 or 5 can play, with the extra player or players sitting out in each deal so that only 3 play at a time)

Cards
32, with all the cards below seven (except the Aces) removed from a 52-card pack. (You can also buy special German or French Skat decks.)

When a suit is declared trumps, the ten ranks above the King in all four suits. In addition, all four Jacks become trump cards and players can score points on them. The four trump Jacks are ranked in order: clubs (high), spades, hearts, then diamonds (low).

To win
Bid to name the game then score the most points.

To deal
The players cut the cards to decide the first dealer. The dealer shuffles the cards and presents the pack to the player on his or her left to cut it.

Starting with the player on his or her immediate left, the dealer deals out the cards in packets as follows: three to each player, two on the table, four to each player then a final set of three to each player, making a total of ten cards in each hand.

Players take it in turns to deal the cards, with the deal passing to the left each time.

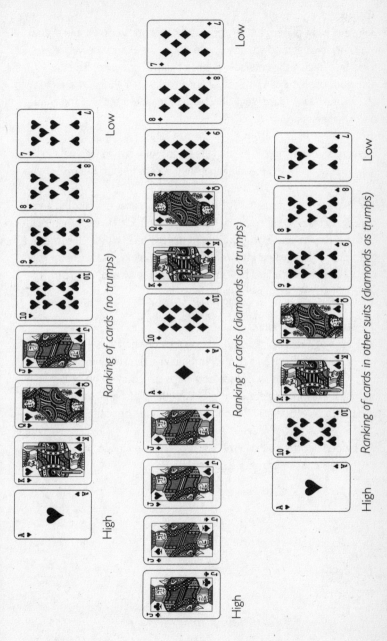

Ranking of cards (no trumps)

Ranking of cards (diamonds as trumps)

Ranking of cards in other suits (diamonds as trumps)

To bid

Before playing, players bid to decide which player will play solo against the other two and how many points he or she expects to win in tricks in a declared game (see "Types of game" opposite). The minimum bid is 18 card-points taken in tricks with a usual maxiumum of around 100. A player may also bid to win all ten tricks in the hand or lose every single trick.

Players can either "pass", meaning they do not want to take part in the bidding, or "hold", meaning that they accept the last bid made.

The player to the dealer's left (the first hand) makes the first bid and bids against the player to his or her left (the middle hand). When one of these players passes, the winner of the bid then bids against the third player (the last hand). When there is a winning bidder, he or she can make one more final bid or decide not to play and "pass", in which case the cards are re-dealt.

To play with the skat

The winning bidder picks up the two cards on the table – the "skat". He or she can choose to play with them and discard two cards from his or her hand. (The two discarded cards still count in his or her final score.) If the bidder decides to play with the skat, he or she can only choose to play "Suit" or "Grand", not "Null" (see opposite).

If a bidder decides to leave the skat alone and continue "handplay", he or she can choose any of the games below.

Types of game

There are three main types of game.

Grand: The only trumps in play are the four Jacks, which act like a fifth suit of four cards. Therefore, if a player leads with a Jack, the other players must follow suit with another Jack if possible. In this game, the cards in the other four suits rank Ace, ten, King, Queen, nine, eight, seven and the player aims to take at least 61 points in tricks. If the bidder has chosen to play "handplay", leaving the skat alone, then he or she can also elect to play "open grand" by laying his or her cards face up on the table.

Suit: One suit acts as trumps, plus the four Jacks which rank above the rest of the cards as follows: Jack of clubs, Jack of spades, Jack of hearts, Jack of diamonds, Ace, ten, King, Queen, nine, eight, seven. Again, the bidder aims to take at least 61 points in tricks. As with grand, a player can choose to play "open suit", by playing with his or cards face up on the table.

Null: No suit acts as trumps and the bidder aims to lose every trick in the hand. Cards rank Ace, King, Queen, Jack, ten, nine, eight, seven in all four suits. A bidder playing "handplay" can also choose to play "open null" in which he or she still aims to lose every trick but plays with the cards in the hand face up on the table.

A bidder can increase his or her score in the game before leading with the first card by calling "schneider", which is a bid to take 91 card-points in tricks, or "schwarz", which is a bid to win every trick in the hand.

To play

The first hand leads by placing his or her first card face up on the table. The other two players must try to follow suit if possible. If a player cannot follow suit, then he or she can play a trump card if a trump suit has been declared by the bidder, or discard.

The card of the highest leading suit, or the highest trump card if played, wins the trick. The winner of the trick leads the first card of the next trick, and so on, until all ten cards have been played.

To score
Points are awarded according to the values of cards won in tricks.

11 points – any Ace

10 points – any ten

4 points – any King

3 points – any Queen

2 points – any Jack (if trumps are declared)

(Nines, eights and sevens have no points value)

Points are also awarded according to the type of game played, as follows:

23 points – simple null game

24 points – open null game

Suit games (the value of which is multiplied by a "multiplier" – see below)

12 points – clubs

11 points – spades

10 points – hearts

9 points – diamonds

24 points – grand games (the value of which to be multiplied by a "multiplier" – see below)

36 points – open grand

Multipliers
A player adds together all his multipliers to get a total ranging from 2 to 14, then multiplies this number by the value of the base game. Multipliers are as follows:

1 for the number of matadors held or not held (see opposite)

+1 for making a game

+1 for a schneider (when the bidder takes at least 90 points)
+1 for a schwartz (when the bidder wins every trick)
+1 for handplay (not using the skat)
+1 for a schneider declared (handplay only)
+1 for schwarz declared (handplay only)
+1 for playing an open suit (declaring all the cards and winning all the tricks)

Matadors

Matadors are the highest consecutive trump cards held by the bidder starting with the highest, the Jack of clubs If the bidder holds the Jack of clubs, then he or she is said to be playing "with (a certain number of) matadors". If he or she does not, then he or she is said to be playing "without (a certain number of) matadors".

Bidder is playing "with one matador" (holds the Jack of clubs but not the Jack of spades in his or her ten-card hand) and multiplies the game value by one.

Bidder is playing "with two matadors" (holds the Jack of clubs and the Jack of spades but not the next consecutive Jack, the Jack of diamonds) and multiplies the game value by two.

Bidder is playing "with three matadors" (holds three Jacks but not the fourth in the sequence) and multiplies the game value by three.

Bidder is playing "with four matadors" (holds all four Jacks) and multiplies the game value by four. (Note: four is the maximum in a "grand" hand with the player being able to hold up to eleven matadors in a suit game.)

Bidder is playing "without one matador" (holds the Jack of spades but not the higher card, the Jack of clubs, in his or her ten-card hand) and multiplies the game value by one.

Bidder is playing "without two matadors" (holds the Jack of hearts but not the Jack of spades or the Jack of clubs) and multiplies the game value by two.

Bidder is playing "without three matadors" (holds the Jack of diamonds but not the other three, higher, Jacks) and multiplies the game value by four.

The value of the game is only affected by the number of matadors in a hand, whether or not the player holds them ("with") or does not hold them ("without").

Skat cards can be included in a matador, even if the bidder does not use them during the hand.

To score the scat

When all the tricks have been played, the points value of the skat cards (or the value of the discard cards if the skat was already taken by the bidder in a suit or grand game) can be included in the score. The skat is discarded in a null game.

To make the bid

A player makes his or her bid if the number of points won in the game are more than or the same as his or her opening bid. If he or she is successful, the number of points won is added to his or her total score.

If the player fails to make the bid, then he or she loses the whole value of the game (the number of points bid) and the amount is deducted from the player's total score. If the player used the skat cards, then he or she loses double the value of the game. If the bidder fails to win at least 31 points, the bidder is said to be "schneidered" and the value of the lost game is increased by an additional multiplier (to be agreed) before being doubled then deducted from his or her total score.

At the end of the game over several deals, the scores are added up and the player with the highest score wins.

Solo

Solo whist, or Solo, became popular in Britain at the end of the 19th century as a change from partnership whist. It is usually played with four players for stakes. It is no longer as popular as it once was having been overtaken by Bridge (see page 51).

Solo

Difficulty rating
3

Number of players
4

Cards
52, with Aces ranking high

To win
Take or lose a certain number of tricks bid at the beginning of the hand.

To deal
The cards are cut to decide who deals and the dealer shuffles the cards and deals them all out face down in four sets of three followed by one final card so that each player has thirteen cards in total.

The dealer turns up his or her last card to show the trump suit for the hand and the card remains face up on the table until the player's bids have been made. After the auction, or bids, the dealer takes the card back into his or her hand before the first card is played.

To bid
Each player takes it in turn to bid, starting with the player on the left of the dealer. Each player's bid must be higher than that of the previous player, otherwise the player can "pass".

Bids in the auction are as follows, starting with the lowest bid:

"Pass" – No bid. If all four players pass, the cards are shuffled and re-dealt by the next player. Usually, if a player passes, he or she cannot bid again. However, if a player passes, the next player proposes (see below) and the following two players pass, then the first player is allowed to "cop", or take the offer of partnership.

"Prop" or "Propose" – A bid offering to join with another player in a partnership to take eight tricks in total. If a player proposes and none of the other three players accepts, then the player can change his or her bid to "solo" (see below). If he or she decides not to bid "solo", then the cards are re-shuffled and re-dealt.

"Cop" (or **"I'll take you"**) – An acceptance of a "prop". A player cannot accept a prop if another player has made a higher bid.

"Solo" – A bid to take five tricks and play alone against the other three players.

"Misère" (or **"Mis"**) – A bid to take no tricks at all. If a player bids "misère", then the hand is played without a trump suit.

"Abondance" – A bid to make nine tricks with the trump suit being changed to a suit chosen by the bidder. (Note: The bidder does not need to declare the chosen trump suit until he or she is sure that the bid has won the auction.)

"Abondance in trumps" – A bid to make nine tricks with the trump suit staying the same as the turned up card on the table. (This bid is usually only made after a player bids "abondance".)

"Misère ouverte" (or a **"spread"**) – A bid to take no tricks at all (as misère) but with the bidder placing all his or her cards face up on the table after leading with the first card. If a player bids misère ouverte, then the hand is played without a trump suit.

"Abondance déclarée" (or a **"slam"**) – A bid to take all thirteen tricks in the hand without a trump suit with the caller leading with the first card of the game.

The highest bid wins the auction.

To play

The player to the left of the dealer leads the first trick unless the highest bid is "Misère ouverte" or "Abondance déclarée", where the caller leads.

Tricks are won following the normal rules of whist with the winner of each trick leading the next. The players must follow suit if they can. If they cannot, they can discard or play a trump card.

A hand ends with the bidder, or caller, winning his or her bid or conceding defeat. In a similar way, the bidder's opponents can also concede defeat without playing every trick in the hand.

To score

Scores can either be kept on paper or the game can be played for stakes, which should be agreed at the beginning of the game. If playing for stakes, usually everyone pays into the kitty at the beginning of a hand and when everyone passes. Stakes should be pre-agreed for each bid. For example one counter could be paid to each winner by each loser for "prop" and "cop", or two counters from each player should be paid to a successful bidder, and so on. Higher calls, such as "abondance" or "abondance in trumps" could be paid at a higher rate.

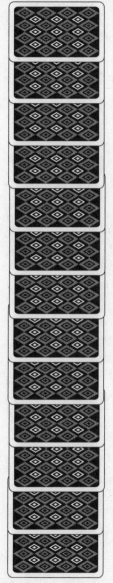

13 cards per player

Trump – turned up by the dealer (last card)

Spoil Five

Spoil Five is the national card game of Ireland and is usually called Twenty-Five. It takes time to learn the scoring value of different cards but once played it can be addictive! The game is probably around 400 years old and is best played with five players.

Spoil Five

Difficulty rating
2

Number of players
2–10 (but best played with 5)

Cards
52, with the ranking of cards changing from suit to suit (see illustration opposite). In the ranking of cards for the black suits – clubs and spades – the two is higher than the ten, whether each suit is plain (not trumps) or the trump suit. When any of the four suits is the trump suit, the highest card is the five of that suit, followed by the Jack, then the Ace of hearts.

To win
Take at least three tricks or all five if possible, or "spoil" all five tricks by preventing any other player from taking three or more.

To deal
Before the dealer deals, each player puts an agreed amount into the kitty. (Each player usually has 20 counters and antes one counter into the kitty, or pool, before each deal.)

The cards are cut to determine the first dealer, with Aces counting high and two low. The player cutting the lowest card deal first.

Starting with the player to the dealer's immediate left, each player is dealt five cards each, in packets of two then three, or three then two.

The dealer leaves the stock face down on the table and turns the top card of the stock face up to determine trumps.

Clubs and spades:

Plain suit, not trumps

Trumps

Diamonds and hearts:

Plain suit, not trumps

Trumps

To rob the trump

If the turned-up card is an Ace, then the dealer can "rob" the Ace – taking it into his or her own hand and exchanging it for another card (which is discarded face down). The trump suit determined by the Ace still stands. If the turned-up card is not an Ace, then any player holding the Ace of the trump suit can rob the trump before playing a card in the first trick.

If the player holding the trump Ace does not wish to rob the turned-up card and does not tell the other players that he or she is holding the trump Ace before playing a card in the first trick, then the Ace, whenever it is played, counts as the **lowest** trump card.

To play

The player to the dealer's immediate left plays the lead card of the first trick, and the winner of each trick plays the first card of the next trick.

If the lead card is not a trump, a player can follow suit or play a trump card (even if he or she is able to follow suit). A player can only discard if he or she cannot follow suit.

If the lead card is a trump, a player must follow suit if possible. However, players can "renege", or hold back, any of the top three trumps held (the five, Jack and the Ace of hearts) if the lead card is a lower trump. For example, if the lead card is the nine of trumps, a player holding the five, Jack or Ace of hearts need not play it. However, if the lead card is a trump five, then the player holding no other trump than the Jack or the Ace of hearts has to play it to the trick. Similarly, if the lead card is a trump Jack, then the player holding no other trump but the Ace of hearts must play it. (Note, however, that if the player holding the Ace of hearts did not announce the fact at the beginning of the deal, the Ace counts as the lowest trump card.)

To jinx

A player winning the first three tricks can either claim the counters in the pool, or he or she can "jinx" by leading the first card of the fourth trick. If a player jinxes in this way, he or she has to win all five tricks.

To spoil

If none of the players wins three tricks or if a player tries to jinx and only wins three or four tricks rather than all five, then the game is said to be a "spoil". Each player then antes another counter into the pool which is then carried over to the next deal. If a player wins three tricks, he or she can claim the pool. If a player wins all five tricks, he or she can claim the pool plus an extra counter from each of the other players.

Whist

Whist is an old card game that first became popular around 1750. It is derived from an even earlier game called Ruffs and Honours which, in turn, found its origins in a game called Trump. There are several kinds of Whist including Solo Whist, Nomination Whist and Knockout Whist. The most prestigious of all is perhaps Bridge (see page 51).

Basic Whist

Difficulty rating
1

Number of players
2–4

Cards
52, with Aces ranking high

To win
Take the most tricks.

To deal
The cards are shuffled then cut to decide the dealer, with the player holding the highest card making the first deal.

The dealer deals seven cards to each player, one card at a time. He or she then turns up the next card to decide trumps. The rest of the pack is placed face down on the table.

To play
The player to the immediate left of the dealer, or the dealer's opponent if just two people are playing, leads with his or her first card. The other player or players must follow suit if possible. If a player cannot follow suit, he or she can either discard or play a trump card. The highest card of the leading suit wins unless a trump card is played, then the trump card wins the trick. If two trump cards are played, then the highest trump takes the trick.

The player taking the most tricks wins the game.

(Also see **Knockout Whist** on page 347.)

Partnership Whist

Difficulty rating
2

Number of players
4, playing in partnerships

Cards
52

To win
Take the most tricks.

To deal
The cards are shuffled then cut to decide partnerships. The two players cutting the two highest cards play together in one partnership, and the two cutting the lowest cards play together in the other. Partners sit opposite each other.

The dealer deals 13 cards to each player, starting with the player on his or her immediate left.

To choose trumps
To choose trumps, either the dealer turns up the next card in the pack and leaves it on the table so all the players can see it, or he or she turns up the last card of the deal (that is, his or her thirteenth card). He or she then takes that card into his or her hand and play begins. The method of choosing trumps should be agreed at the beginning of the game.

To play
The player sitting to the immediate left of the dealer leads the first trick by playing any card. The other players must play a card of the same suit if possible. If they cannot, they can either discard or play a

trump card. Each trick is won by the highest card in the leading suit or by the highest trump card if a trump has been played.

The winner of a trick plays the lead card of the next trick.

Won tricks are placed face down on the table in front of one of the players in each partnership. Tricks should be overlapping crosswise so that each batch of four cards is grouped together and can be counted easily.

The game continues in the same way until all 13 tricks have been played.

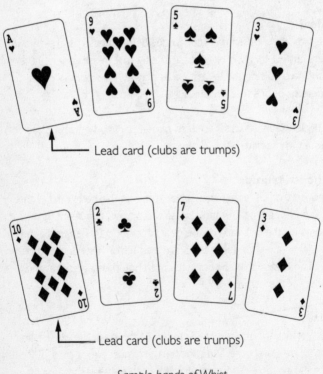

Lead card (clubs are trumps)

Lead card (clubs are trumps)

Sample hands of Whist

The illustration on page 208 shows two sample hands of Whist, played early in a game. The first trick is won by the lead card, the Ace of hearts, with the second and last player following suit and the third player discarding a card because he or she does not hold a heart and does not need to play a trump (because it is likely that his or her partner who played the Ace will win the trick).

The second trick is won by the two of clubs, with the last two players having to follow suit. From this, the first player learns that his or her partner does not hold any diamonds higher than the ten, otherwise he or she would have played them to win the trick.

A revoke is caused when a player does not follow the leading suit even when he or she can play a card in that suit. If this is a mistake, it can be corrected by playing another card immediately before the trick is turned over. If both partnerships revoke, then the cards are re-dealt. Penalty points are awarded for revokes if the trick is turned over (see below).

To score
There are two main methods of scoring – the English system and the American system. In the United States, the first partnership to reach seven points wins the game. In English Whist, the first partnership to reach five points wins. In both types, the partnership that wins the most tricks scores one game point for every trick won over a total of six tricks. There are three games in a rubber and the whole match is won by the partnership with the most points at the end of a rubber. If the first two games in a rubber are won by the same partnership, then the third and final game in the rubber is not usually played and the partnership winning the two games gets two additional points towards their final score.

Seven-point scoring
• 1 point for every trick won by a partnership over and above a total of six tricks
• 2 points given for a revoke

The final score for each game is the difference between seven and the total score of the losing partnership. Usually, the final hand is played out even after one partnership reaches a total of seven points and any extra points are added to the total score.

Five-point scoring

In English Whist, points are also scored for "honours" (the Ace, King, Queen and Jack of the trump suit).

• 1 point for every trick won by a partnership over and above a total of six tricks (called a "book")

• 2 points if one partnership has won tricks containing three honours (any three of the Ace, King, Queen and Jack of trumps)

• 4 points if one partnership has won tricks containing all four honours (the Ace, King, Queen and Jack of trumps)

(If two honours have been taken by each partnership then neither side scores.)

• 3 penalty points for a revoke. (These are either lost by the partnership that revokes, gained by their opponents or transferred from the partnership that revokes to the other partnership. The ruling on awarding penalty points must be agreed at the start of the game.)

As with seven-point scoring, the final hand is played out even after one partnership reaches a total of five points and any extra points are added to the total score (with the winners getting three additional points if the opposing partnership scores nothing, two points if the opposing partnership has one or two points, and one point if the opposing partnership has three or four points).

Although Whist is easy to learn, great skill lies in choosing which cards to play to win the most tricks. Skilled players become good at sending and receiving signals from one another. These signals are sent according to which cards are led and discarded in tricks. For example, if the partner of a player who has led a trick plays a high card (that is, higher than a six) it means that the player likes the suit that his or her partner led with and probably has some good cards in that suit that could win tricks. However, if the partner plays a low card to the lead card it usually means that the player doesn't like his partner's leading suit and would prefer another suit to lead the next trick.

In a similar way, signals can also be sent when discarding cards. For example, if a player discards a high card it usually means that the player has some good cards in the discarded suit and wants an opportunity of playing them. If a player discards a low card it means the player is interested in other suits and has few good cards in the suit of the discarded card.

Progressive Whist

Progressive Whist is usually played at Whist Drives. It is played in the same way as Partnership Whist but with players changing tables and partners at every deal. In Progressive Whist the dealer does not turn up a card for trumps. Instead, the suits rotate for each hand in the following order: hearts, clubs, diamonds, spades.

Dummy, or Three-Hand Whist

Dummy Whist is the most popular version of Whist for three players. The three players cut the cards to decide which player has the "dummy", which is a fourth hand dealt and laid out on the table and played by one of the players as well as his or her own hand. The person with the lowest cut card wins the dummy for the whole of the first rubber, the next lowest cut card wins it for the second rubber and the third wins it for the third and final rubber. The two players without the dummy hand play as partners during the rubber.

The player with the dummy hand deals the cards, with the dummy hand being dealt second, across the table from the dealer. The dealer turns the cards in the dummy hand face up and arranges them into suits and plays from it as if it is his or her partner in the game.

Contract Whist

Contract Whist is the same as Partnership Whist except that players bid to name the trump suit and win a certain number of tricks.

To bid

After the cards have been dealt, the player immediately to the dealer's left starts the bidding to name the trump suit and win a certain number of points as follows:

1 point – requires the partnership to take six tricks plus an additional trick to make the point bid

2 points – requires the partnership to take an additional two tricks over the "book"

3 points – requires the partnership to take an additional two tricks over the "book", and so on up to

11 points – (the highest bid) – requires the partnership to take six tricks to make the "book", the remaining seven tricks and all four honour cards (the Ace, King, Queen and Jack of the trump suit named by the bidder).

Each bid made must be higher than the previous bid. If a player bids and the other three players pass, then the bidder announces trumps, wins the contract and plays the lead card of the first trick. As with basic Whist, players must follow suit if possible. If they cannot, they can either discard or play a trump card. The highest card in the lead suit wins unless a trump card has been played in which case the trump card wins the trick. If two or more trump cards are played then the highest trump wins the trick.

Nomination Whist

Difficulty rating
2

Number of players
3–7 (but best played with 4–5)

Cards
52, with Aces ranking high

To win
Bid to take a certain number of tricks and then win exactly that number.

To deal
The cards are cut to decide who deals and the player with the lowest card deals first. Cards are dealt face down, singly, starting with the player to the immediate left of the dealer. The dealer should deal out all the cards so that each player has an equal number. If any cards are

left over, the dealer places them face down on the table and turns up the top card to decide trumps. If no cards are left because the cards divide equally between the players, then the game is played with no trumps.

To score

The scorekeeper keeps the score by ruling a sheet of paper into columns, with one column for each player. Each player's initials are written at the top of each column. The scorekeeper writes down how many tricks each player proposes to take in each hand and the total number of tricks that it is possible to win (according to the number of cards).

To play

The player to the immediate left of the dealer starts by bidding how many tricks he or she hopes to take. The lowest bid is "none" with the player saying "None" or "Pass" and the highest is the maximum number of tricks possible with the player's total number of cards.

The player to the immediate left of the dealer leads with the first card. The rest of the players must follow the suit if possible. If they cannot, they can either discard or play a trump card (if there are trumps being played in the hand). As with other games of Whist, a trick is taken by the highest card in the leading suit or by the highest trump, if any trumps are played.

To score

Any player who takes the exact number of tricks that he or she bid scores a point for each trick plus an additional ten points. Any player who does not take the exact number of tricks bid "busts" and scores nothing. The scorekeeper writes down each player's score and keeps a running total, by adding up each player's score after every hand.

Players take it in turn to deal the cards, shuffling them before each deal. At each deal, however, the number of cards in each hand decreases by one. After every deal, the next card in the pack is turned up for trumps. On the final deal of the game, each player is only dealt one card and no card is turned up for trumps.

The winner is the player with the highest score after all the deals in the game.

(Also see **Solo**, page 193)

Card Games
for One

Patience, or Solitaire, is a group of games designed for just one player. In most games, the player deals out the cards in a certain way then attempts to put them back in order, usually so the cards are in sequences by suit. Some games of Patience are won solely by luck; others require skill to help you beat the cards. The following section includes most well-known games of Patience and a few more unusual ones, too. Difficulty ratings have been awarded according to whether the game is easy or difficult to win.

Accordian

Difficulty rating
3

Cards
52

To win
Get all the cards in one pile, or stack.

To deal
Shuffle the cards well then deal out the cards in a row, face up, from left to right. You can either deal out all 52 cards in one go if you have plenty of room, or deal out just four or five to start with if space is limited. If you are dealing out the cards a few at a time, deal slowly so that you don't miss any possible moves.

To play
Move one card on top of another card to its immediate left or third on its left (that is, the next but two) if it matches in number or suit. If there is more than one card in the stack, move all the cards in the stack together. Only match the single cards and the cards on top of each stack.

It's almost impossible to get all the cards in one stack. Award points depending on how many stacks are left after all possible moves have been made. Anything under ten is pretty good. Three or less is amazing!

In this game of Accordian, the Queen of diamonds can be moved on top of the six of diamonds because it's the same suit. The ten of spades then moves up and the next card – the eight of hearts – is dealt.

Now the eight of hearts can move over the eight of clubs three to its left and another new card is dealt.

The new card – the seven of spades – can be placed over the ten of spades to its immediate left, then the stack (both the ten and the seven) can be moved over the seven of diamonds three to the left, as shown below.

The next move could be to place the next card dealt – Queen of spades – over the seven of spades three to the left or over the Queen of diamonds to its immediate left. At this point, it's difficult to tell which move will work out best.

Auld Lang Syne

Difficulty rating
3

Cards
52

To win
Build the cards into four sequences of 13 cards each, starting with the Aces and ending with the Kings.

To deal
Remove the four Aces from the pack and lay them in a row then deal four cards face up in a row underneath from left to right.

To play
If any of the first four cards dealt is a two, then play it on its Ace. A three can then be played on the two, and so on. Once any possible moves have been made, deal another four cards over the top of the first four or into any gaps to make up a row of four, and again make any possible moves. Keep moving and re-dealing until the whole of the stockpile has been exhausted. You can only play a card when it is at the top of one of the piles or when it has been exposed by having played the card covering it.

This game is almost impossible to get out. Building cards in sequences regardless of suit improves the odds, as does dealing six cards in a row instead of four.

Foundation row
(Aces)

None of the first four cards dealt can be moved up so the player deals four new cards over the top of them. In this row, the player can move up the two and three of diamonds and the two of spades. However the three of spades cannot be played until the seven of diamonds — and any card or cards that are dealt on top of it — are played first.

Betsy Ross or Four Kings

Difficulty rating
2

Cards
52

To win
Build up the four foundation cards into sets of 13 cards.

To deal
Remove any Ace, two, three and four from the pack and place them face up on the table in a row, from left to right.

Then remove any two, four, six and eight from the pack and place them face up in a second row. These make up the foundation row. Shuffle the rest of the cards. These form the stock.

To play
Build up the four foundation cards, each in a different way.

Build up the two under the Ace by ones, that is:
2, 3, 4, 5, 6, 7, 8, 9, 10, Jack, Queen, King

Build up the four under the two by twos, that is:
2, 4, 6, 8, 10, Queen, Ace, 3, 5, 7, 9, Jack, King

Build up the six under the three by threes, that is:
6, 9, Queen, 2, 5, 8, Jack, Ace, 4, 7, 10, King

Build up the eight under the four by fours, that is:
4, 8, Queen, 3, 7, Jack, 2, 6, 10, Ace, 5, 9, King

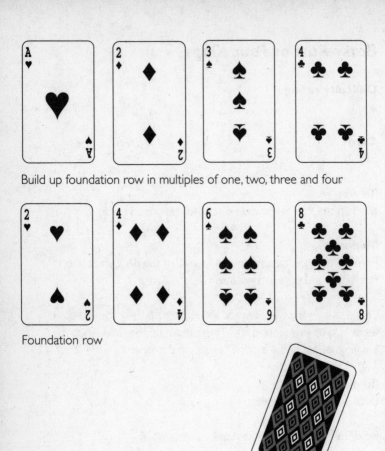

Build up foundation row in multiples of one, two, three and four

Foundation row

Tableau for Betsy Ross

Stockpile

Go through the stockpile one card at a time and play any card you can to the second foundation row. (The top row of cards is simply to remind you how to build on each foundation card.)

You are allowed two more deals. If all the cards "come out" you will be left with a row of Kings under the Ace, two, three and four.

Broken Intervals

Difficulty rating

I

Cards

52

To deal

Remove any Ace, two, three and four from the pack and place them face up on the table in a row, from left to right.

The rest of the pack becomes the stock.

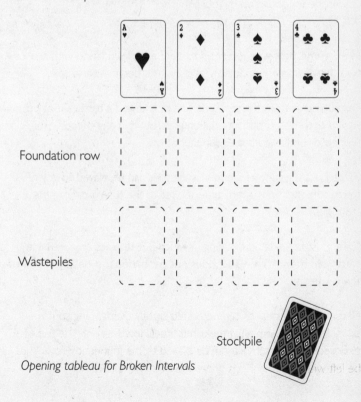

Foundation row

Wastepiles

Stockpile

Opening tableau for Broken Intervals

To play

This game is played in the same way as Betsy Ross (see page 223), with each of the foundation cards being built up to Kings in sequences, as follows:

Under the Ace, build up by ones, that is:
2, 3, 4, 5, 6, 7, 8, 9, 10, Jack, Queen, King

Under the two, build up by twos, that is:
2, 4, 6, 8, 10, Queen, Ace, 3, 5, 7, 9, Jack, King

Under the three, build up by threes, that is:
6, 9, Queen, 2, 5, 8, Jack, Ace, 4, 7, 10, King

Under the four, build up by fours, that is:
4, 8, Queen, 3, 7, Jack, 2, 6, 10, Ace, 5, 9, King

In this game, however, you need to start each foundation with an Ace, two, three or four respectively as soon as it becomes available.

Turn up cards from the stockpile one at a time. If a card cannot be played onto one of the foundation piles, put it in any of four wastepiles underneath the foundation row.

The top card of any of the four wastepiles can be played to any of the four foundations at any time, as well as the top card from the stockpile.

Care must be taken in deciding in which pile to place any unusable card from the stockpile so it does not get buried too deeply in one of the wastepiles.

Cards in the wastepiles can be placed slightly overlapping so it is possible to see them all at the same time. However, only the top, exposed card in each pile can be played to the foundation row.

Keep running through the pack placing cards directly on the foundations or temporarily in the wastepiles until no further moves are made or the cards "come out" and are built up to four Kings.

Clock Patience I

Difficulty rating
3

Cards
52

To win
Build all the cards into a clock face, with the four Kings in a pile in the centre of the clock.

To deal
Shuffle the cards, deal them into thirteen equal piles of four, and arrange them into the shape of the numbers on a clock face with the thirteenth pile in the centre.

To play
Turn over the top card of the central pile of four and put it in its corresponding place on the clock face, then take the next card from that pile and put that in its place on the clock, and so on. For example, if the first card is a three, place it in the position of three o'clock and

take the top card of the pile of four in front of the three and put that in its corresponding position. Jacks are positioned at 11 o'clock, Queens at 12 o'clock, and Kings are placed in the centre.

To win
Complete the clock face before you draw the fourth and final King.

Cheat's Version of Clock Patience
Placing each King at the bottom of a different pile of four means the game comes out more often than not!

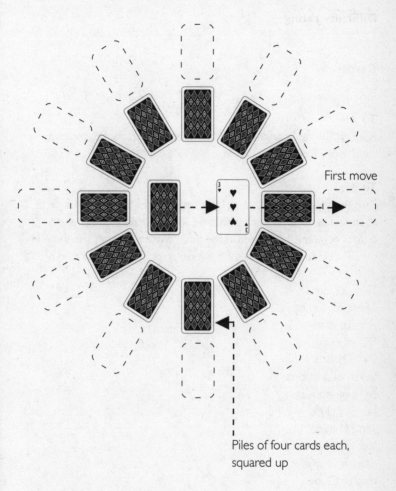

First move

Piles of four cards each, squared up

Opening formation of Clock Patience I

Clock Patience II

Difficulty rating
I

Cards
52

To win
Build up the cards on the clock face so that the clock resembles a "real" clock face.

To deal
Take the following cards out of the pack and set them out in a circle, as shown in the illustration opposite, with the nine in the twelve o'clock position, the Queen in the three o'clock position, the three in the six o'clock position, the six in the nine o'clock position, and so on.

Two of hearts
Three of diamonds
Four of spades
Five of clubs
Six of hearts
Seven of diamonds
Eight of spades
Nine of clubs
Ten of hearts
Jack of diamonds
Queen of spades
King of Clubs

(You can choose to remove other suits as long as there are three sets of cards of each suit on the clock face.)

Deal out the rest of the pack of cards in rows of eight, slightly overlapping the cards so that you can see all the cards in the tableau.

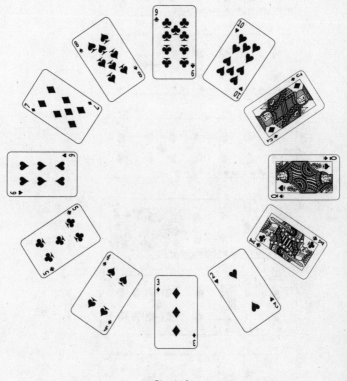

Clock face

Opening tableau for Clock Patience II

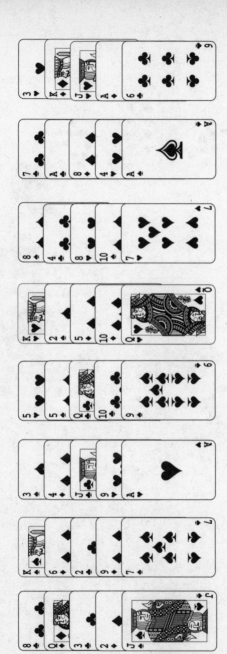

Clock Patience II

To play

Build on the exposed cards on the tableau downwards in sequence, no matter what suit they are, so in the tableau opposite, the Jack of spades can be moved onto the Queen of hearts.

At the same time, remove any cards to the clock face, building them up by suit and in sequence, so the six of clubs can be moved onto the five of clubs, and the nine of spades onto the eight of spades.

Keep building up cards onto the clock face where possible. To free cards for building, move cards on the tableau either singly or in sequences.

When all the cards in a column on the tableau have been used up, move a King or a sequence with a King at the top into the space to free another card underneath.

If all the cards "come out", then the cards in the clock face will resemble a "real" clock face with the Queen at the top in the twelve o'clock position, and so on.

There will be four cards in each pile on the left side of the clock face from the six o'clock position to the Queen, and five cards in each pile on the right side of the clock face from the one o'clock position to the five.

Completed tableau for Clock Patience II with the Queen at the top and the rest of the cards in their "real" positions on the clock face.

Cross or Corners

Difficulty rating
2

Cards
52

To win
Build the four corner foundation cards upwards by rank into 13-card suits.

To deal
Deal out five cards in the shape of a cross to form the tableau, as shown in the illustration overleaf.

Turn up the next card from the pack and place it at the top left-hand corner of the tableau to start the first foundation.

To play
Play any cards if possible from the cross to the foundations, building upwards by suit.

At the same time, play any cards onto others within the cross building downwards and regardless of suit. For example, in the tableau overleaf, either of the two nines can be placed on the ten.

Fill any gaps in the cross with cards from the stock.

When any possible moves have been made to the foundations or within the cross, start going through the stock, one card at a time. If a card cannot be played, place it in a wastepile.

Kings can be placed on Aces in the tableau, and Aces can be placed on Kings in the foundations.

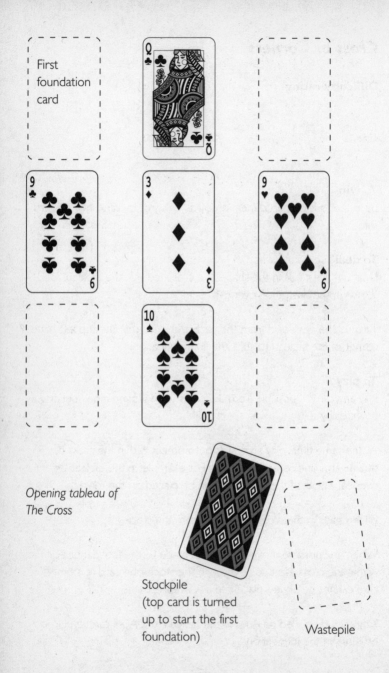

First foundation card

Opening tableau of The Cross

Stockpile
(top card is turned up to start the first foundation)

Wastepile

When you have been through the stock, you can play the cards in the wastepile, starting with the top card. You can only play the card beneath once the top card has been moved to the foundations or the tableau.

Demon or US Canfield

Difficulty rating
3

Cards
52

To win
Build up all the cards into sequences by suit or use up as many cards as possible from the "demon" pile.

To deal
Deal out thirteen cards face down in a pile and turn the top card face up. This is the "demon" pile. Deal the next card face up to start a foundation row of four cards. Under this card, deal out four more cards in a row to start the layout, or tableau.

To play
Build the cards on the tableau in downward sequences of alternating colours. For example, a red Jack can be placed on a black Queen, and a black ten on the red Jack, and so on. At the same time, build on each foundation card in suits following the first card. For example, if

Example of a sequence starting with a five.

If a gap is made in the tableau by moving a card or a sequence of alternating cards, then the top card of the demon pile can be moved over to fill the gap.

Once all possible moves have been made, turn up cards from the stockpile in sets of three, playing the top card if possible, then the second, then the third. If no cards can be played, turn over another set of three cards, and so on. Once the cards from the stock have been used up, turn the whole pile face down and go through it once more, again dealing in sets of three. There is no limit on the number of times you can go through the pile of stock.

Demon rarely comes out so it is fun to count the number of cards left in your demon pile at the end of the game and try to better your score.

the foundation card is a five of hearts, then the next card to be played on it must be a six of hearts, and so on, and the other three sequences in the foundation row must also start with fives.

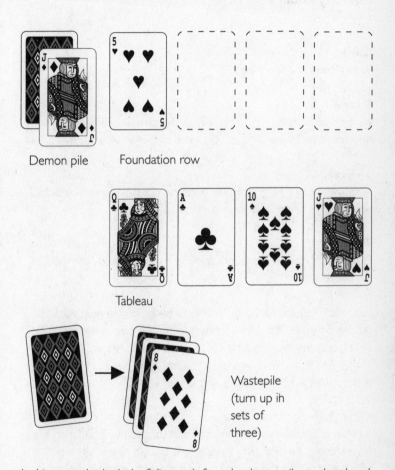

Demon pile   Foundation row

Tableau

Wastepile
(turn up in
sets of
three)

In this example, the Jack of diamonds from the demon pile can be played onto the Queen of Clubs. The top card from the demon pile is then turned face up. If that card is a five, it can be played onto the foundation row at the top and the next card in the demon pile can be turned up. The ten of clubs can be played onto either of the red Jacks, and a new card from the demon pile can be put in its place to make up the row.

Double or Quits

Difficulty rating

I

Cards

52, removing the four Kings

To win

Build up one single foundation until all the cards in the pack have been used up by doubling the pip value of the previous card.

To deal

Remove the four Kings from the pack then deal out seven cards face up as shown in the illustration opposite.

To play

Each card played to the foundation pile must be double the value of the previous card.

For example, if the foundation card is a two, then the next card that can be played on it is a four. Similarly, if the top card in the foundation card is a three, then the next card that can be played on it is a six.

In the game, Jacks count as 11, and Queens as 12.

When doubling arrives at a figure of more than 12, subtract the number of cards in the suit and add that card to the foundation pile. For example, if a card just played is nine, double nine is eighteen, minus thirteen, so the next card to be played to the foundation should be a five.

For example, if the foundation card is a Queen, you would need to place cards on it in the following sequence:

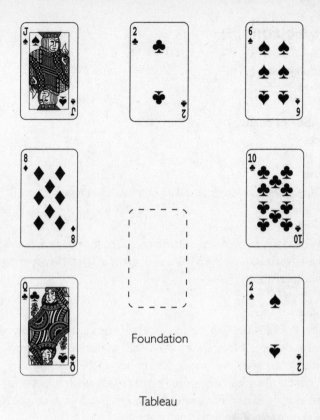

Foundation

Tableau

Opening tableau of Double or Quits

Turn up the next card and place it in the centre. This is the foundation card and all the other cards in the pack will be built on this.

The rest of the cards form the stock.

Stockpile (Top card is turned up to start the foundation pile)

Double Fan

Difficulty rating
I

Number of cards
2 packs

To win
Build the foundation cards into suits from Aces to Kings.

To deal
Deal out all the cards in sets of three and place them in fans, face up on the table. This will make 34 fans with two cards left over, forming its own set of cards.

To play
As with Fan Patience, only the top, exposed cards in each fan can be played at any time. Move any exposed Aces to the foundation row and start building up the cards in suits on top of them. At the same time, start building on the exposed cards in each fan in suits. Cards can be built in upward or downward sequences but Kings cannot be played on Aces, nor Aces on Kings.

Double Fan Variation
In another version, again played with two packs of cards, the foundation row is made up of eight Aces and eight Kings. Exposed cards from the fans are built upwards on the Aces and downwards on the Kings, by suit.

(Also see **Fan Patience** on page 243.)

Fan Patience or La Belle Lucie

Difficulty rating
2

Number of cards
52

To win
Build the foundation cards into suits from Aces to Kings.

To deal
Deal out all the cards in sets of three and place them in fans, face up on the table. The remaining single card forms its own set.

To play
Only the top, exposed cards in each fan can be played. Move any Aces to the foundation row, to start building up the cards in suits. Any exposed twos can be placed on the Aces, and threes on the twos, and so on, following suit. At the same time, cards can be built on each fan, also by suit, in downwards sequences, so the five of diamonds can be placed on the six of diamonds, or the Jack of spades can be placed on the Queen of spades, and so on. When all the cards in a fan have been used, the space is not re-filled.

When no more moves are possible, gather up all the cards in the fans, shuffle them, and re-deal them, again in fans of three. Any leftover cards form sets of one or two. Only one re-deal is allowed.

Special Grace
One "grace" move is allowed. This can either be to move a King in one of the fans to the bottom of its pile at the beginning of the game (to give the game a better chance of coming out), or to exchange any two cards in a fan at any point during the game.

(Also see **Double Fan** on page 242.)

Foundation row

Opening tableau for Fan Patience

In the game of Fan Patience illustrated opposite, the Ace of diamonds and the Ace of spades are exposed at the top of fans and can be moved to the foundation row. The five of diamonds can be moved onto the single six, then the two of spades can be moved out to the foundation row, and so on.

Flower Garden

Difficulty rating
1

Cards
52

To win
Build up the four Aces, by suit, to Kings.

To deal
Deal out six cards in a row face up from left to right, then deal out a further five rows of cards on top of the first, with all the cards slightly overlapping to make the "flower garden".

Place the remaining sixteen cards in a row, face up, at the bottom of the tableau, as shown in the illustration on page 246.

To play
Move any exposed Aces from the bottom of the tableau or from the row of sixteen stock cards to the foundation row, then start building on the Aces upwards by suit.

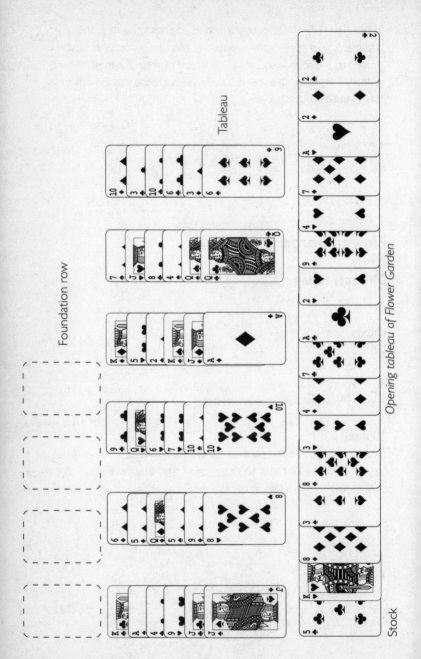

Tableau

Foundation row

Opening tableau of Flower Garden

Stock

— 246 —

Any of the cards in the row of stock can be played at any time. They do not need to be played in order.

To free cards within the tableau for moving to the foundation row, build on any exposed cards in the tableau downwards in alternate colours, so a red Jack can be placed on a black Queen, and so on.

If any of the six spaces within the tableau becomes free, you can move up a King or a sequence of cards with a King at the top.

Keep moving single cards or sequences of cards within the tableau and build up the foundations until no further moves are possible or the game comes "out" and the four Aces are built up to Kings in sequence by suit.

Fourteen Out

Difficulty rating
1

Cards
52

To win
Discard all the cards in the pack in pairs that total 14.

To deal
Shuffle the cards and deal out a row of 12 cards face up. Deal out a further three rows of cards on top of the first row slightly

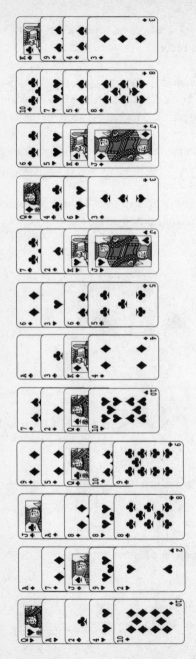

Opening tableau for Fourteen Out

overlapping. Place the remaining four cards over the first four columns, so the layout looks like the illustration opposite.

To play

Remove any two, exposed, cards that add up to 14, as follows:
Ace and King (worth 13)
2 and Queen
3 and Jack
4 and 10
5 and 9
6 and 8
7 and 7

Keep pairing cards until you can no longer make any pairs or you can pair them all.

Gaps or Spaces

Difficulty rating
3

Cards
52

To win
Arrange four rows of cards into sequences running from twos to Kings in the same suit.

To deal
Deal out the whole pack of cards face up in four rows of 13 cards each from left to right, as shown in the illustration on page 250.

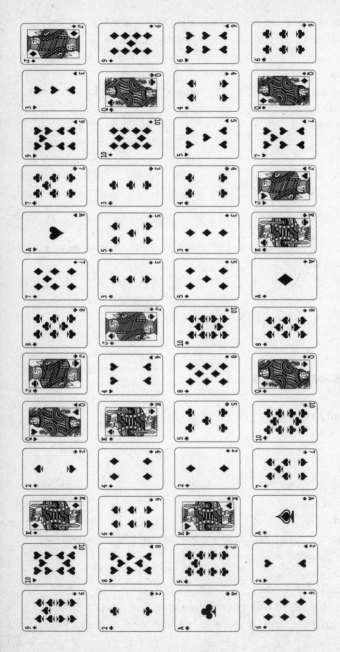

Opening tableau of Gaps

To play

Remove the four Aces and discard them, leaving four gaps or spaces in the rows.

Fill any gaps in the layout by a card that is the same suit and the next higher in rank than the card to the left of the gap.

For example, in the tableau on page 252, after discarding the four Aces, the eight of diamonds can be moved into the gap on the top row, to the right of the seven of diamonds. In the same way, the three of hearts and the nine of spades can be moved into the gaps on the bottom row.

Any gaps left on the far left of the tableau can be filled by any of the four twos.

Keep moving cards to fill in gaps, always keeping four rows and no more than 13 cards in a row.

When a King lies to the left of a gap, then the gap cannot be filled and no more cards can be moved on that row. When no further moves are possible in any of the four rows, gather up all the cards that are not in the correct sequence and suit (excluding the Aces), as shown in the illustration on page 253. Shuffle the cards and deal them out so that there is a gap to the right of each sequence.

If the only card in the correct place in a row is a two, leave a gap to its immediate right.

If a row does not have a two in it, leave a gap at the beginning of the row so that a two can be moved into it.

Continue playing in the same way until no further moves can be made, then gather up any cards not yet in position, shuffle, and re-deal.

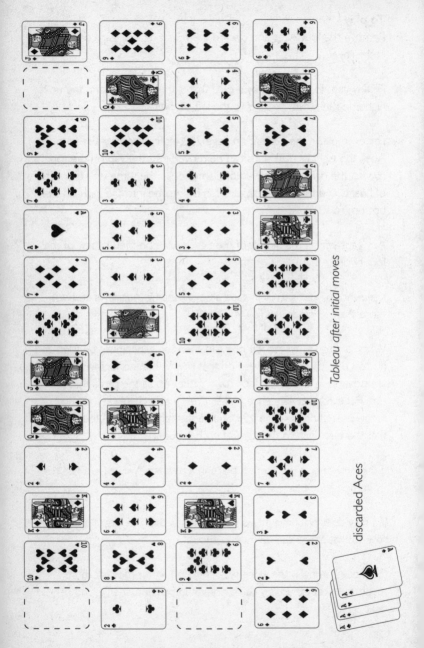

Tableau after initial moves

discarded Aces

— 252 —

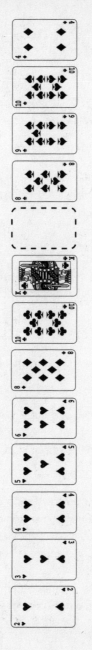

When re-dealing, leave the hearts sequence from two to six in position and shuffle the cards in the rest of the row in with those from other rows. When re-dealing the cards, leave a gap to the right of the six of hearts.

Either allow yourself as many deals as necessary or limit the redeals to two.

Glenwood or Duchess

Difficulty rating

1

To win

Build up the foundation row into suits of 13 cards each.

To deal

Deal out four sets of three cards and arrange them into fans, as shown in the illustration opposite.

Leaving a space for the foundation row, deal out a row of four cards.

Choose one of the exposed cards in the fans to start the first foundation row.

In the tableau opposite, for example, you could choose the Queen of clubs to start a foundation row because you can immediately move the Queen of hearts from the tableau to start another foundation pile, then place the King of hearts from the third fan on top of it.

To free cards from the tableau so you can move them to the foundations, build downwards in sequences on cards in the tableau, in

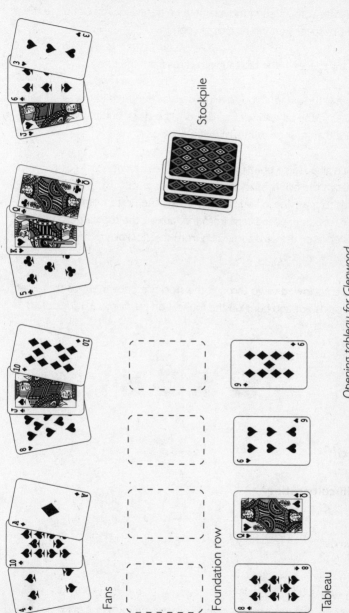

Fans

Foundation row

Tableau

Stockpile

Opening tableau for Glenwood

alternate colours, so in the example on page 255, you can place the eight of spades on the nine of diamonds.

Fill any spaces in the tableau with cards from the fans.

Later in the game, if you have used up all the cards in the fans, fill any spaces in the tableau with cards from the stock, but always having no more than four cards in a row at any time.

Once all possible opening moves have been made, start going through the pile of stock one card at a time, discarding any unusable cards to a wastepile. You can play an exposed card from any of the four fans, an exposed card from the tableau, the top card from the wastepile or the card turned up from the stockpile to the foundation row at any time.

You are allowed to go through the stockpile once more to try to get the cards out and build up the foundation cards into full suits of 13 cards each.

Golf

Difficulty rating
3

Cards
52

To win
Build up all the cards into a single pile, starting with a dealt base card.

Or, to use golfing terminology, sink the remaining 51 cards into the base card "hole".

To deal
Deal out seven cards in a row, face up. Deal a further seven cards face up on top of this row, slightly overlapping, then another row of seven, and so on, until you have five rows in total. Turn the next card face up and place it on one side of the tableau to form the base card, or "hole".

To play
Move cards on top of the base card whether they are higher or lower in rank, no matter what suit they are. So, if the base card is a five, you can put a four or a six onto it of any suit. Sequences end with an Ace or a King, so you cannot play an Ace on a King or vice versa to continue a sequence.

Any of the exposed cards in the tableau can be played onto the base card. If there are no possible moves to be made using cards in the tableau, turn over the top card from the stockpile and put it on the foundation card and continue to build sequences of cards from there.

If all the cards in a vertical column are "sunk" into the hole, then a new column is not formed. The game is over when all the cards are played into the "hole".

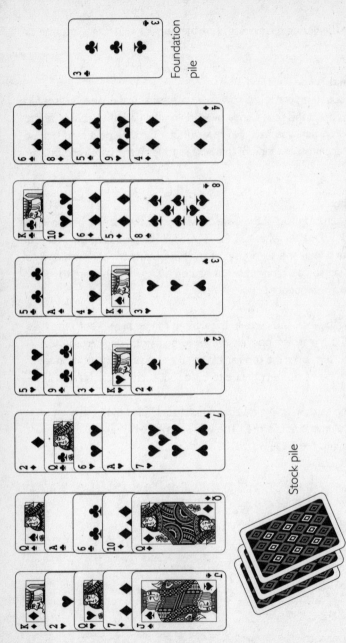

Foundation pile

Stock pile

The opening moves in this game of Golf could be to place the four of diamonds onto the three of clubs in the foundation pile, followed by the two of spades then the three of hearts. Once all possible moves have been made, the top card is turned up from the stock pile.

Intelligence

Difficulty rating
3

Cards
Two packs

To win
Build up the foundation row by suit, from Aces to Kings.

To deal
Deal out 18 fans, with three cards in each fan. As you deal, place any Aces that appear straight on the foundation row.

Place the rest of the cards in a pile, as the stock.

To play
Move any exposed cards at the end of each fan to the foundation row, if possible.

At the same time, move cards within the tableau by building on the exposed cards at the end of each fan either upwards or downwards, by suit.

For example, in the tableau on page 260, you could move the two, three and four of diamonds and two twos, one three and one four of spades straight to the foundation row.

You could then move the seven of diamonds or the nine of diamonds onto the eight of diamonds within the tableau, and so on.

You can change the direction of a sequence within each fan if necessary.

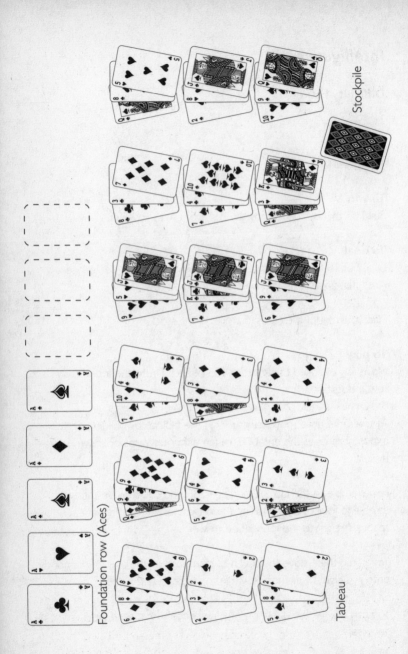

Foundation row (Aces)

Tableau

Stockpile

Once you have used up all the cards in a fan you can deal out three new cards from the pile of stock. As you deal out the new cards, move any Aces that appear straight to the foundation row.

Once all possible moves have been made, gather up all the cards in the fan, shuffle them with the cards in the stockpile and re-deal them into eighteen fans, again with three cards in each fan.

As you re-deal, move any Aces that appear to the foundation, as before.

You are allowed one more re-deal (two re-deals in total) to try to beat the cards.

Klondike or English Canfield

Difficulty rating
3

Cards
52

To win
Build the cards into four sequences following suits, from Ace to King.

To deal
Turn up one card then deal six more face down in a row alongside from left to right. Turn up another on top of the second card then deal a further six cards face down. Turn up another on top of the

third card then deal out a further five cards face down. Continue dealing until the layout, or tableau, is complete.

To play

Build the cards on the tableau in downward sequences of alternating colours. For example, a red eight can be placed on a black nine, then a black seven on the red eight, and so on. Any exposed Aces are put into a foundation row, at the top of the tableau. These are built up in suits, ending with the Kings. Once a card has been played onto a foundation pile, it cannot be moved.

When a card has been moved, the card underneath is turned up and brought into play. If all the cards in one row are used up, you must leave a gap until it can be filled by a King. There can only be seven rows in the tableau at any time.

Once any initial moves have been made, turn over cards from the pile of stock one at a time and either play them to the foundation row or to the sequences. If a card from the stock cannot be used, then it is placed in a wastepile. The top card in the wastepile can be played at any time during the game.

In a variation of Klondike, cards from the stockpile are turned over in sets of three. The second card in the set can only be played if the top card is played, and the third card in the set can only played if the top two cards are played. Once the stockpile has been used up, the pile can be turned over and re-dealt one more time (twice in some versions).

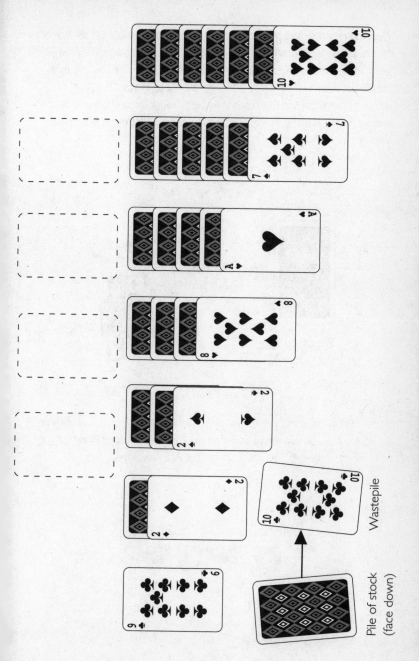

Wastepile

Pile of stock
(face down)

Opening moves in this game of Klondike, would be to move up the Ace of hearts to the foundation row, then move the seven of spades onto the eight of hearts, the seven and eight together onto the nine of clubs and the seven, eight and nine together onto the ten of spades. The four exposed cards the tableau could then be turned face up. Assuming there are no more moves to make, cards are turned over from the wastepile one at a time.

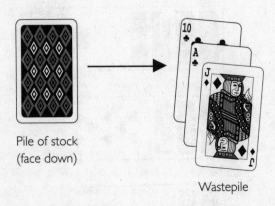

Pile of stock
(face down)

Wastepile

In some versions, cards are turned over from the stock pile in sets of three. Here, the Ace can only be played if the Jack is played first, and the ten can only be played if both the Jack and the Ace are played.

Klondike with Two Packs of Cards

Difficulty rating

I

Cards

Two packs

To win

Build up the foundation row by suit, from Aces to Kings.

To deal

Deal out one card face up then eight cards face down. On the second row, deal one card face up on the first face down card, then seven cards face down. Repeat this for a further seven rows. The layout is the same as that for Klondike, except that there are nine cards in a row instead of seven (see the illustration on page 266).

Move any exposed Aces to the foundations and build on them if possible. At the same time, build on the exposed cards in the tableau downwards in sequences of alternate colours. In the tableau on page 266, for example, you can place the black eight on the red nine, then the red six, black five and red four running downwards on the black seven.

Turn over any exposed cards at the end of the columns and play them to the foundations if possible or move them within the tableau.

Any gaps in the tableau can be filled by a King or by a sequence of cards with a King at the top.

When all possible moves have been made, start running through the pile of stock one card at a time.

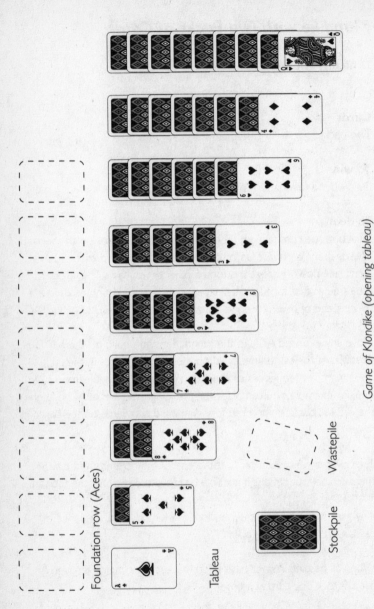

Foundation row (Aces)

Tableau

Wastepile

Stockpile

Game of Klondike (opening tableau)

At any time, you can play the top card from the pile of stock or the top card from the wastepile to the tableau or to the foundation row.

In the illustration of the game of Klondike (with two packs) in progress, the next move would be to place the ten of hearts from the stockpile onto one of the three black Jacks. The nine of clubs from the wastepile could then be placed on the ten and the red eight sequence onto the nine, exposing a face-down card.

Masked Twelve

Difficulty rating
2

Cards
52

To win
Move the cards and build all the cards into suits on the layout, running from Kings at the top to Aces at the bottom (see illustration on page 268).

To deal
Deal out two cards face down, three cards face up, then two cards face down from left to right to form the first row. Repeat this for a further two rows. Then deal out another four rows of seven cards, all face up.

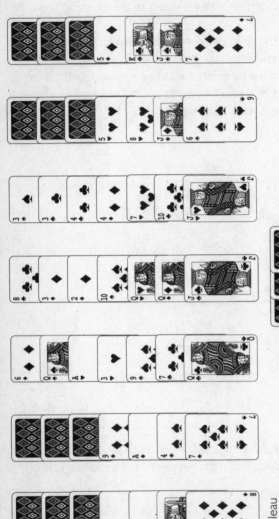

Stock (three cards)

Tableau

Opening tableau of Masked Twelve

— 268 —

Place the three remaining cards face down under the layout.

To play
Move cards around the tableau, building downwards by suit. For example, in the example opposite, you can place the seven of diamonds on the eight of diamonds, and the Jack of clubs onto the Queen of clubs.

As well as moving single cards at the end of each column, you can also move cards within the tableau onto any of the exposed cards. When doing this, you also have to move all the cards underneath the card you are moving as well. For example, in the same tableau, you can move the ten of clubs onto the exposed Jack of clubs but you need to move the Jack of hearts as well. Similarly, when the Jack of spades has been exposed after moving the seven of diamonds, you can move the ten of spades from the fourth column on top of it, along with the cards below.

Any gaps in the tableau can be filled by a King.

Face down cards can be turned up and brought into play when they are exposed at the end of a column.

When no more moves are possible within the tableau, you can turn up the first of the three stock cards to see whether it can be brought into play. Repeat with the other two stock cards when no more moves can be made.

If the cards come out, you will be left with four columns with each suit running down in sequence from Kings to Aces (see illustration on page 270).

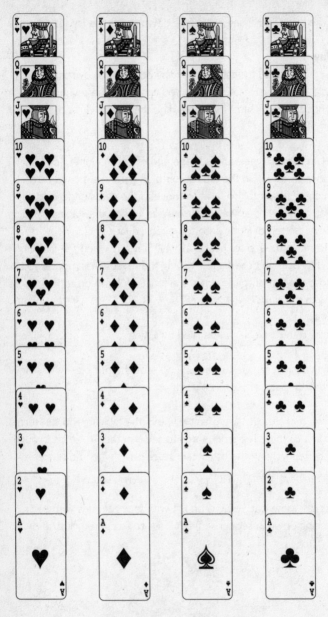

Completed game of Masked Twelve

Matrimony

Difficulty rating
2

Cards
52

To win
Discard all the cards in the pack in pairs of the same rank.

To deal
Shuffle the cards then deal out a row of eight cards face up. Slightly overlapping the first row, deal out another row of eight cards, then another, until there are six rows of cards altogether.

While dealing, keep checking to make sure that there are not two cards of the same rank in any of the vertical columns. For example, if you turn up a Queen onto a column and there is already a Queen in that column, place the Queen underneath the pack of cards and carry on dealing.

When you have finished dealing out the cards, there will be four cards left over. These four cards should be placed underneath the layout, face down.

To play
Collect and discard any two exposed cards of the same rank. When you can no longer pair any cards, turn up the first of the first four cards in the stockpile and see whether that can be used to make a pair with one of the exposed cards in the layout. If it cannot, turn up the second of the four cards, and so on.

Carry on discarding pairs until you can make no further moves or all the cards are paired.

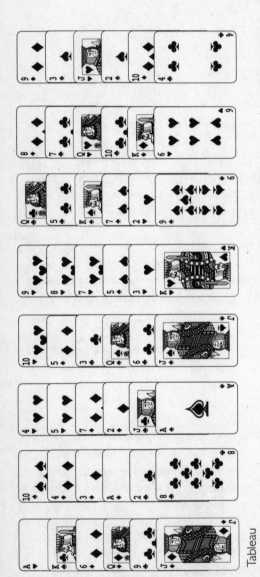

Tableau

Stockpile

The opening moves of this game of Matrimony would be to pair the two Jacks, then the exposed six of clubs with the six of hearts and the exposed nine of clubs with the nine of spades. You could also pair the King of hearts with the King of diamonds. Once no further moves can be made, turn up the first of the face-down cards to try to pair it with one of the exposed cards and carry on making as many pairs as possible.

Miss Milligan

Difficulty rating
3

Cards
Two packs

To win
Build up the cards in the foundation row by suit, from Aces to Kings.

To deal
Deal out eight cards face up in a row. Remove any Aces and place them in the foundation row. If possible, build on any of the Aces in an upward sequence, following suit. At the same time, build on cards in the tableau in a downward sequence by alternate colour, so a red ten can be played onto a black Jack, and a black nine onto the red ten, and so on. Cards can be moved singly, or in sequences. For example, a black nine, red ten and black Jack can be moved together onto a red Queen.

Once no more possible moves can be made, deal out eight more cards in a row across the bottom, exposed cards of the layout, filling in any gaps. Make any possible moves, then deal out a further eight cards on the layout, and so on.

When all the cards in the stockpile have been played onto the layout, and when no more moves can be made, you can try "weaving".

To weave
Choose and remove any exposed card in the tableau and set it on one side. Then make any possible moves to the foundation row or within the tableau, starting with the newly exposed card. Continue making moves until you can no longer play, in which case you have lost the game, or until you can return the single card to the tableau or build it on one of the foundation piles. If you do this, you can remove another single card from the tableau and continue to play as before. Only one card can be removed at any time.

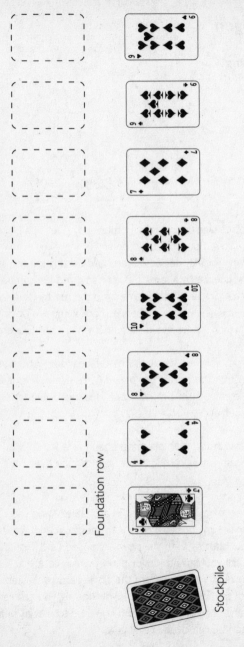

Foundation row

Stockpile

Opening tableau of Miss Milligan. There are no Aces to move up to the foundation row but cards can be built downwards in alternate colours, leaving five gaps (see next page).

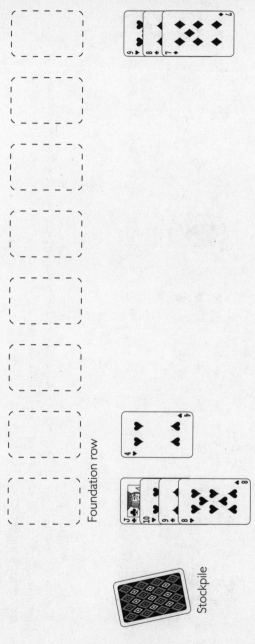

Foundation row

Stockpile

Once no more cards can be moved, another eight new cards are dealt across the tableau from the stockpile (see next page).

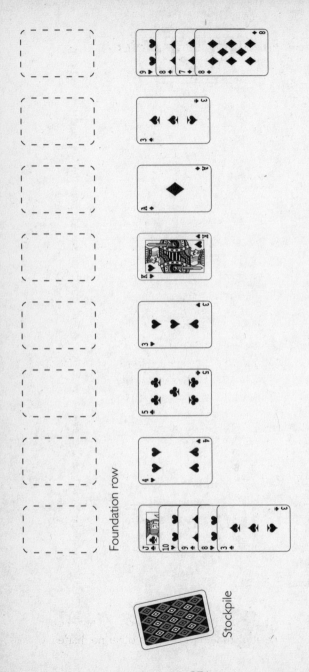

Foundation row

Stockpile

The Ace can now be moved to the foundation row, one of the threes can be played onto the four of hearts, and the three and four together can be placed on the five of clubs. Weaving can only begin when all the cards in the stockpile have been played across the layout.

Napoleon's Favourite or St Helena

Difficulty rating
I

Cards
Two packs

To win
Build four Aces upwards to Kings, by suit, and build four Kings downwards to Aces, by suit.

To deal
Remove one Ace and one King of each suit from the packs of cards and place them in two rows with the Aces under the Kings, as shown in the illustration on page 279, to form the foundation rows.

As if you are dealing out a hand of twelve cards, deal out all the cards one at a time in a clockwise direction starting from the top left-hand corner. Continue dealing out the cards until you have dealt out all the pack. There will be eight cards in each of the piles.

To play
Move as many cards as possible to the foundation piles.

During the first round of the game, any card at the side of the foundations can be moved into the foundation row. Any card in the top row can be moved to the top foundation row (building downwards on the Kings), and any card in the bottom row can be moved to the bottom foundation row (building upwards on the Aces).

(This rule changes on subsequent rounds.)

To free cards for building onto the foundations, you can move cards within the tableau one at a time on top of each other, no matter what suit, either building them upwards or building them downwards, changing direction as many times as required within each pile.

When building, Aces cannot be placed on Kings or Kings on Aces.

Gaps in the tableau cannot be filled with any card or sequence of cards from one of the other piles.

When no more moves are possible, gather up all the piles of cards surrounding the foundation rows, starting with the last pile dealt to in the top left-hand corner and picking up the piles in an anticlockwise direction.

Re-deal the cards as far as they will go, starting with the row of four at the top and dealing them clockwise.

On the second (and third) deal, you can place any card from any position on the tableau onto the foundation rows. Keep moving cards to the foundation row and within the tableau until the cards come out or there are no more possible moves.

You are allowed one final deal (making three in total) to try to get the cards out.

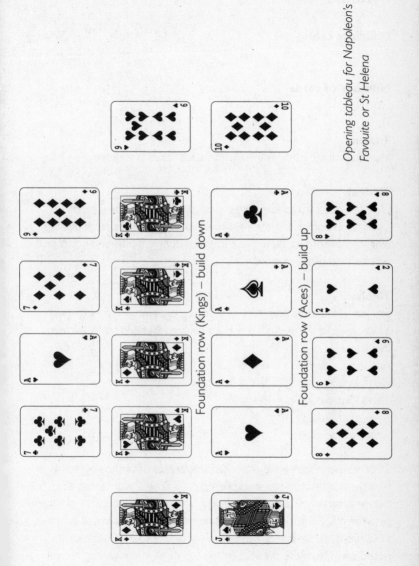

Foundation row (Kings) – build down

Foundation row (Aces) – build up

Opening tableau for Napoleon's Favouite or St Helena

Pyramid

Difficulty rating
3

Number of cards
52

To win
Match up all the cards in the pack to pairs totalling thirteen.

To deal
Deal out one card to form the top of a pyramid, then two cards slightly overlapping it in the next row below, then three cards overlapping the row of two, then four cards overlapping the three, and so on, up to a total of seven rows.

To play
Starting with the bottom row of seven cards, remove any Kings (with a face value of thirteen) or any pairs of cards that add up to thirteen, that is:

Ace and Queen	4 and 9
2 and Jack	5 and 8
3 and 10	6 and 7

Only free, or exposed, cards can be moved from the pyramid.

Once you've discarded as many cards as possible from the pyramid, turn over cards from the stockpile, one at a time. If you cannot use the new card immediately by pairing it with an exposed card from the pyramid, place it in a wastepile, to one side. Keep turning over cards from the stockpile one at a time, making pairs either with the exposed cards from the pyramid or the top cards in the wastepile until you have paired off all the cards in the pack.

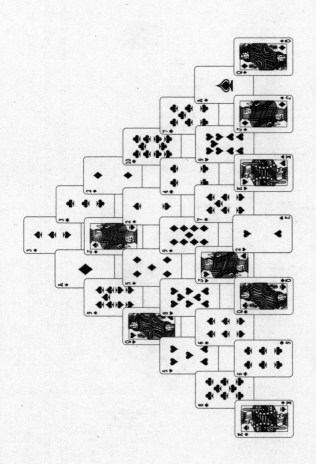

In this game of Pyramid, the two Kings (each with a face value of thirteen), then the Jack and the two (totalling thirteen) can be removed from the bottom row of cards, bringing the seven and the nine from the next row into play. The seven from the sixth row and the six from the bottom row can then be paired, exposing the eight.

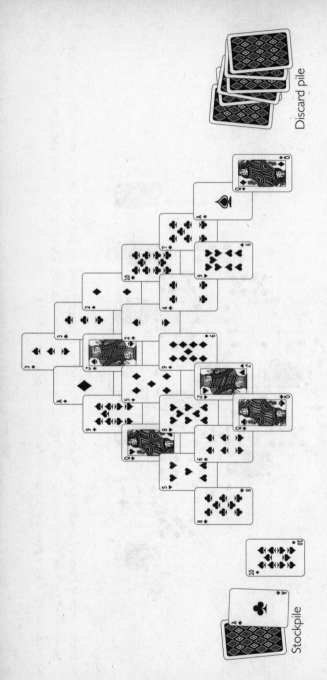

Discard pile

Stockpile

Once all possible pairs have been discarded, the top card is turned over from the stockpile – here, the ten of spades. As it cannot be paired, the next card is turned over, the Ace of clubs, which can be paired with the Queen. New cards are turned over from the stock one at a time. Then ten can be used at any time until covered by another card from the stockpile.

Quadrille

Difficulty rating
I

Number of cards
52

To win
Get all the cards "out" by building on the fives and sixes in sequences and using up the cards in the pile of stock.

To deal
Remove the four Queens, sixes and fives from the pack and arrange them on the table, as shown in the illustration on page 284, with the four Queens in the middle and the fives and sixes placed alternately around them in a circle.

To play
Turn cards face up from the pile of stock, one at a time, and either build them onto the tableau, or put them in a wastepile.

Sequences should be built in suits, as follows:

Once the cards in the stockpile have been used up, the pile can be turned over and re-used. In most versions of Quadrille, you are allowed to turn over the stockpile a maximum of three times to give the game an even chance of coming out.

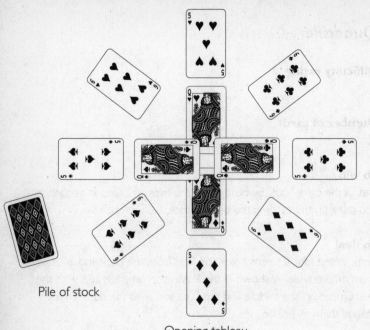

Pile of stock

Opening tableau

Sequences should run downwards on the fives, to the Kings.

Sequences should run upwards on the sixes, to the Jacks.

Queen's Audience

Difficulty rating
I

Cards
52

To win
Build the four cards in the foundation row from Jacks down to twos
in suits.

To deal
Deal out four sets of four cards, face up, to form the sides of a square,
as shown in the illustration on page 286.

To play
Move any Jacks from the walls of the chamber into the centre to start
the foundation row. However, only move a Jack into the centre when
you can move an Ace of the same suit with it at the same time,
placing the Ace under the Jack.

Kings and Queens of the same suit can also be moved into the centre
of the chamber in pairs, placing the Kings underneath the Queens.

Once any possible moves have been made from the walls of the
chamber to the centre, fill in any gaps in the walls with cards from the
stockpile. Make any further moves then go through the stockpile, one
card at a time, playing any possible cards to the foundation row or to
make up the pairs of Queens and Kings.

Keep making any possible moves until the cards come out so that the
Jacks are built downwards by suit to twos.

Stockpile

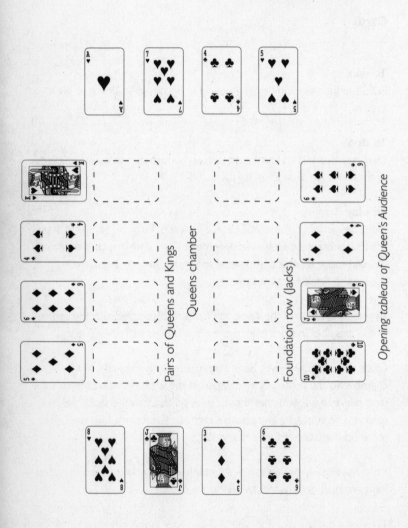

Pairs of Queens and Kings

Queens chamber

Foundation row (Jacks)

Opening tableau of Queen's Audience

Royal Cotillion

Difficulty rating
2

Cards
Two packs

To win
Build all the foundations (starting with an Ace and a two of each suit) upwards into a sequence of 13 cards (see below) each.

To deal
Deal out three rows of four cards, all face up, from left to right.

Leave a space for two cards (for the foundation rows), then deal out four rows of four cards, all face up, as in the illustration on page 289.

To play
Move an Ace and a two of each suit to the foundation rows in the middle of the layout when possible.

The foundation cards should each be built up in twos, by suit.

The Aces should be built up by suit in a sequence running Ace, three, five, seven, nine, Jack, King, two, four, six, eight, ten and Queen.

The twos should be built up by suit in a sequence running two, four, six, eight, ten, Queen, Ace, three, five, seven, nine, Jack and King.

You can move any of the cards from the right-hand part of the tableau onto the foundations. Initially, however, you can only move the bottom four cards from the left-hand part of the tableau onto the foundations. The cards in the second row only become available for building when you have moved all four cards in the bottom row.

Similarly, the cards in the top row can only be played when you have moved all four cards in the middle row.

Any gaps that appear in the left-hand part of the tableau are not filled in. Any gaps that appear in the right-hand part can be filled in with cards from the stockpile.

When any possible moves have been made to the foundations, go through the cards in the stockpile one at a time, moving them onto the foundations if possible or putting them in a wastepile.

Russian Patience

Difficulty rating
3

Cards
52

To win
Build the foundation row from Aces to Kings by suit.

To deal
In the first row, deal out one card face up then six cards face down. In the second row, deal out one card face up on top of the first face-down card then a further five cards face down. In the third row, deal out one card face up on top of the second face-down card then a further four cards face down.

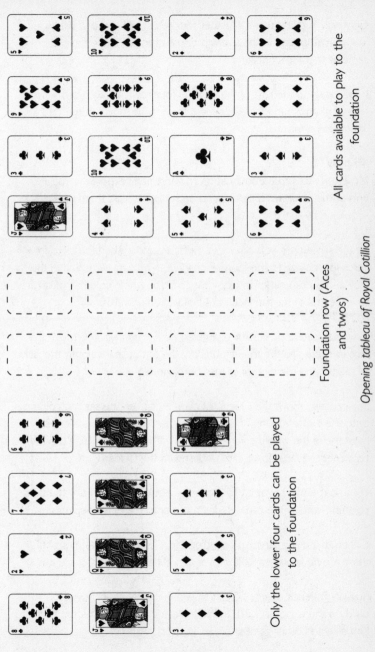

Only the lower four cards can be played to the foundation

Foundation row (Aces and twos).

All cards available to play to the foundation

Opening tableau of Royal Cotillion

— 289 —

Continue in this way for a further four rows until you end with a single face-up card in the seventh row. At this point, the tableau is the same as that for Klondike.

Next, deal out the rest of the cards in four rows, all face up, on top of every column in the tableau except the first, as shown in the illustration opposite.

To play
Move any Aces to the foundation row from any exposed cards at the end of the columns in the tableau, and start to build them upwards in sequence, by suit.

At the same time, you can move cards around in the tableau to free cards for moving to the foundations. When moving cards within the tableau, you can either move single cards, or whole columns of cards to link cards of the same suit but building downwards.

In the tableau opposite, for example, you can immediately move the Ace of spades to the foundation row, the ten of spades onto the Jack of spades and the nine of spades onto the ten.

You can also move the Queen of diamonds from the second column onto the exposed King of diamonds. When doing so, however, you must move the whole column of cards with the Queen. You can then turn over the face-down card underneath the Queen.

Your next move might be to move the eight of spades from the third column – and all the cards beneath it – onto the nine of spades.

Continue moving cards and building cards on the foundations until there are no more possible moves or until all the cards "come out".

Russian Patience is very difficult to win. A slightly easier version is to build on the exposed cards in the tableau in alternate colours, as for Klondike and other games.

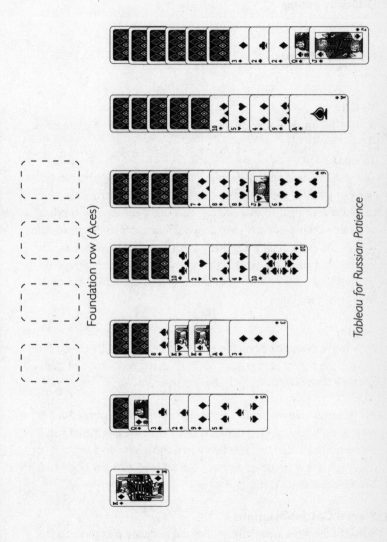

Tableau for Russian Patience

Foundation row (Aces)

Sieged Castle

Difficulty rating

I

Number of cards

52

To win

Build all the cards in suits on the foundation piles, from Aces to Kings.

To deal

Take out the Aces and lay them in a row, going downwards. Now deal out four cards to the left of the Aces, downwards in a row, leaving space on their right so that you can deal out a further four overlapping cards on top of each. Then deal out four cards to the immediate right of the Aces, again going downwards in a row. Next deal out another four cards on the left column, overlapping them slightly, then another four cards on the right column and so on, until all the cards have been used up.

To play

Only the exposed cards on the ends of each row can be played. Build any exposed cards on the Aces upwards in suit, so the two of clubs can be played on the Ace of clubs, and so on.

At the same time, cards can be moved singly or in sequences at the ends of each row, building downwards by rank, irrespective of suit. Therefore, a ten can be played on a Jack and a nine on a ten, and so on. When a row becomes empty, it can be filled with any single card or any sequence of cards.

Sieged Castle Variations

• Shuffle the Aces in with the rest of the pack and play them to the foundations only when they are exposed at the end of a row. When dealing, place seven cards in the top two rows rather than six.

• Shuffle the Aces in with the rest of the pack. When dealing, any Ace that appears can be played immediately to the foundation row. If a two of the same suit is then dealt, it too can be played immediately to the foundation row, and so on. If a card can be moved to its foundation when dealing, leave its space on the tableau empty and continue dealing out the rest of the cards. Once cards have been placed on the tableau during dealing, they cannot be moved until all the cards have been dealt and they are exposed during play.

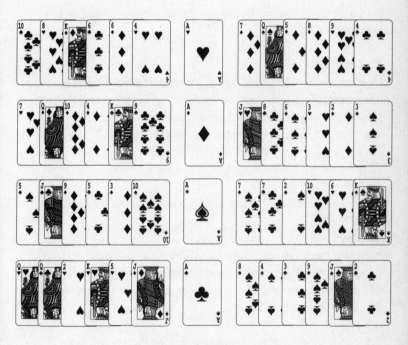

Foundation row

Spider

Difficulty rating

3

Cards

Two packs

To win

Build all the cards within the tableau into sequences running downwards from Kings to Aces.

To deal

Deal out a row of ten cards face down, then deal out another four rows on top. Finally deal out an extra card on top of each of the last six piles. You will therefore end up with five cards in each of the first four piles and five cards in each of the next six piles.

Turn the top card in each pile face up.

The rest of the pack should be put on one side as the stockpile.

To play

Move any cards within the tableau, building downwards as far as possible by suit. Single cards can be placed on other cards regardless of suit. However, groups of cards can only be moved as a sequence if they are in the same suit.

If any gaps appear, you can fill them with any card or a sequence of cards if it is made up of cards of the same suit.

Once all possible moves have been made, deal out ten new cards from the stockpile face up on top of the tableau.

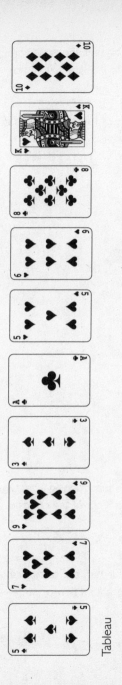

Tableau

Stockpile

Opening tableau of Spider

Keep making any possible moves and re-dealing until the game comes out and all eight Kings have been built down to Aces, by suit, or no further moves are possible.

Once you have built up a complete sequence of 13 cards and you do not need to use any of the cards to help you build up another sequence, discard them. You win if you end up with no cards left on the table.

Spiderette

Difficulty rating
2

Cards
52

To win
Build up the cards in the foundation row into suits, running from two Aces of one colour through to Kings and two Kings of the opposite colour to Aces.

To deal
Deal out four cards face up in a row then a further four cards face up in a second row, leaving space in between for a third row of cards – the foundation row.

While dealing, you can move any cards from the top row of four straight to the foundation row. However, you can only move a card from the bottom row of four straight to the foundation row if that card is directly underneath its position in the foundation row.

For example, if you have turned up an Ace of spades in the first four cards dealt you can move it straight to any position in the foundation row. However, if you turn up a two of spades in the second row of four cards, you can only move it on top of the Ace if the two is directly below the Ace.

Make any possible moves to the foundation row while dealing until the tableau is complete.

To play
Deal out a further eight cards in two rows on top of the other cards in the tableau. At this stage in the game you can move any card from any position in the tableau onto the foundation row.

The base cards in the foundation row can be two red Aces and two black Kings or two black Aces and two red Kings. For example, in the illustration on page 298, you can move either the King of hearts or the Ace of diamonds to the foundation row, but not both.

To free cards for building onto the tableau, move cards singly within the tableau so they run upwards or downwards in sequence, regardless of suit. For example, a black seven can be placed on any six or eight. However, it is usually better to build sequences downwards within the tableau to make it easier to build the foundation cards up.

When building, a King can be placed on top of an Ace.

Any spaces that are made in the tableau cannot be filled.

Foundation row – two Aces of the same colour and two Kings of another colour

Opening tableau for Spiderette

Keep making any possible moves then keep dealing out the cards until they have all been dealt. Then continue moving cards within the tableau and from the tableau to the foundation row. If the game comes "out", the foundation row will be built up to two Kings and two Aces, by suit.

The Sultan or The Harem

Difficulty rating
I

Cards
Two packs

To win
Build up the Ace of hearts and the Kings by suit until the King of hearts in the centre is surrounded by his harem of Queens.

To deal
Remove the Ace of hearts and the eight Kings from the packs of cards.

Place the King of hearts in the centre with the Ace of hearts above it and the other seven Kings around the outside, as shown in the illustration opposite.

Shuffle the cards and deal out eight cards face up, four on each side of the foundation cards.

To play
Move any of the eight cards from the tableau to build on the Ace of hearts and all the Kings except the King of hearts, upwards by suit. In the game illustrated opposite, for example, you can move the Ace of diamonds onto one of the two Kings of diamonds.

Fill in any gaps in the tableau immediately with a top card or cards from the stockpile.

Once any possible opening moves have been made, go through the stockpile one card at a time, placing any cards onto the foundation cards as they appear.

Fill any gaps in the eight cards surrounding the foundation cards immediately with the top card from the wastepile or the card just turned up from the stock.

Once you have run through the stock once, shuffle the cards well and go through it again. You are allowed two re-deals.

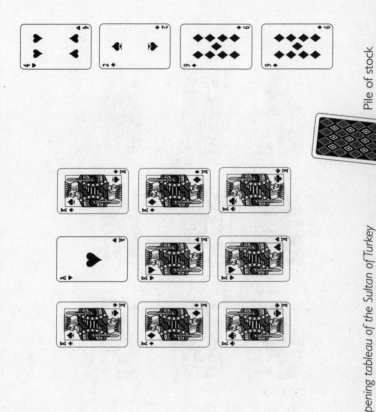

Pile of stock

Opening tableau of the Sultan of Turkey

If the cards "come out", you will end up with the King of hearts surrounded by his harem of queens, as shown in the illustration below.

Completed tableau for The Sultan – the King of hearts surrounded by his harem of queens.

Terrace or Queen of Italy

Difficulty rating
I

Number of cards
Two packs

To win
Build up all the cards in sequences, by suit, from their foundation cards (eight in total).

To deal
Deal out a row of eleven cards, each slightly overlapping the first. Then deal out three more cards underneath. Based on the cards in the terrace, choose one of these three cards to be a foundation and move it up to start the foundation row just beneath the terrace. Then deal out a further seven cards alongside the remaining two cards to form a row of nine cards in all.

To play
Move any card from the tableau or an exposed card at the end of the terrace to the foundation row, building the cards upwards in suits in alternating colours so there are 13 cards in each sequence. If the foundation card is not an Ace, then an Ace can be moved onto a King to continue the sequence. For example, if the foundation card is a Jack, then the sequence runs Jack, Queen, King, Ace, two, three, four, five, six, seven, eight, nine, ten.

At the same time, cards can be played on the tableau in downward sequences of alternate colours. For example a black six can be moved onto a red seven, and a red King can be moved onto a black Ace, and so on.

Once all possible moves have been made, turn over cards from the

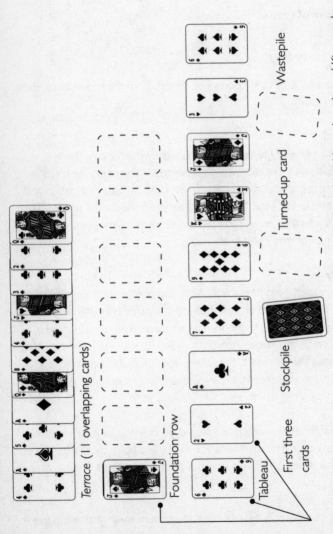

Terrace (11 overlapping cards)

Foundation row

Tableau

Wastepile

Turned-up card

Stockpile

First three cards

The Jack of diamonds can be moved up to the foundation row from the tableau, then the red King can be moved onto the black Ace and one of the black sixes onto the red seven. No more moves are possible, so the top card from the stockpile must be brought into play.

stockpile one at a time. If they cannot be played, put them in a wastepile, face up.

A newly turned up card from the stockpile, the top card from the wastepile, an exposed card from the tableau or the last card in the terrace can be played to the foundation row at any time. If a gap appears in the tableau, fill it in with a card from the stockpile or the top card of the wastepile to make up a row of nine. You are not allowed to add more cards to the terrace.

Thirteen or Baroness

Difficulty rating
3

Cards
52

To win
Discard all the cards in the pack in pairs that total 13.

To deal
Shuffle the cards and deal out a row of five cards face up.

To play
Remove any Kings (each worth 13) or any two cards that add up to 13, as follows:
Ace and Queen
2 and Jack
3 and 10
4 and 9
5 and 8
6 and 7

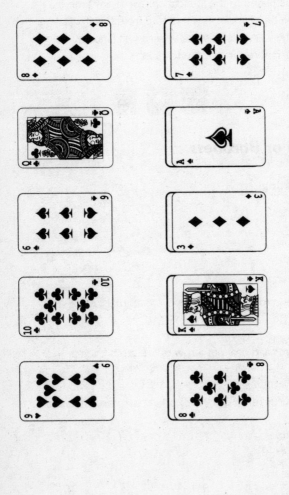

Thirteen or Baroness — no card can be discarded from the first five cards dealt (top). However, from the second row of five cards, the King (worth 13) can be discarded, then the uncovered ten and the three of diamonds. The six of spades is then exposed and can be paired with the seven of spades.

Place any pairs in a discard pile, then deal out a further five cards on top of the first row of cards.

Again, discard any pairs that add up to 13. Only the top, visible cards can be used to pair up cards.

Keep dealing out cards in rows of five until there are two cards left. These two cards can be paired and discarded if possible.

Treasure Trove

Difficulty rating
2

Cards
52

To win
Build up the foundation row of cards into suits but in any sequence.

To deal
Deal out a row of three cards face down then a fourth card face up, all slightly overlapping. Deal out a second, third and fourth row underneath in the same way.

Turn up the next card from the pack and place it to the right of the top pile of cards to start the foundation row.

To play
Each of the other three foundation rows must start with the same

rank card as the turn-up card. In the example opposite, this is the ten of spades. The next foundation rows can only therefore be started with tens.

Build up the cards in the foundation row in suits but in any sequence.

First, move any other cards to the foundation row from the tableau if possible, and turn up any exposed cards, moving them across too if it is possible to do so.

When no moves are possible, go through the stockpile, turning over the cards in sets of three and playing the top card if possible to the foundation row. If the top card in a set of three can be played, then the card exposed beneath can then be played if possible.

A card can only be moved to the second, third or fourth foundation rows if there is a card of that rank already placed in the top foundation row.

For example, if on going through the stockpile, you turn up another ten, such as the ten of clubs, you can place it below the ten of spades. You can do the same with either of the other tens. If you turn up any of the other spades when running through the stockpile, you can also move them straight to the foundation row at the top, no matter what order they appear.

If you then turn up another club, you can only play it to its foundation row if a spade of the same rank has already been played to its foundation row. (See illustration on page 310.)

Treasure Trove Variation

In another version of Treasure Trove, you can deal out the cards so that the face-down cards are all face up so they are all visible, as shown in the illustration on page   .

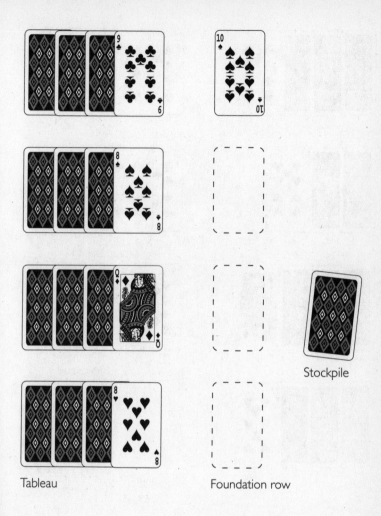

Tableau

Stockpile

Foundation row

Opening tableau of Treasure Trove

Stockpile

Tableau

Foundation row

Turn over
cards in sets
of three

In this game of Treasure Trove, the Queen of clubs that has been turned
up from the stockpile can be moved to the foundation row next to the
ten of clubs because the Queen of spades has already been played to the
row above. However, neither the nine of clubs nor the Queen of diamonds
can be moved to their respective foundation rows because there is no
nine in the spade row at the top and there is no Queen in the clubs row.

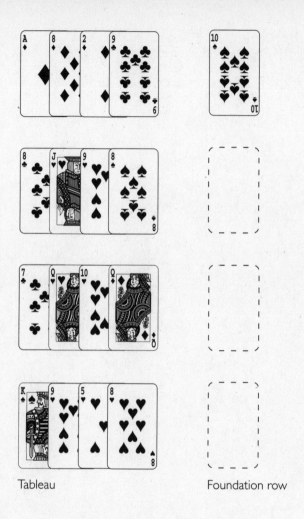

Tableau

Foundation row

Treasure Trove Variation

Children's Card Games I

(for younger children)

The games on the following pages are particularly good for young children but also great fun for older members of the family or simply the young at heart. They're also an excellent way of teaching youngsters skills of matching and counting!

Animals

Difficulty rating

I

Number of players

3–6 (but best with 5–6)

Cards

Two decks

To win

Capture all the cards.

Choosing an animal

Each player chooses the name of an animal, such as DUCK-BILLED PLATYPUS or TYRANNOSAURUS REX. The harder and longer the name is to say, the better. If there are very young players in the game, then long animal names can be written on separate pieces of paper and put into a hat. Each player then takes out a name and must be that animal for the duration of the game. Players must remember the names of the other players' animals.

To deal

The dealer deals out all the cards. It does not matter if they do not come out evenly.

To play

Each player puts his or her stack of cards face down on the table. Starting with the youngest player or the player to the left of the dealer, players take it in turns to turn over the top card of their stack.

If a card matches another in rank (such as two tens or two Kings), then the first player to notice must call out the name of the other player's animal three times as fast as possible. If he or she does this correctly, the player wins the other player's stack of cards and adds it to the bottom of his or her own pile. If he or she calls out the wrong animal name, then the stack of cards must be given to the player whose animal name was called.

The winner is the first person to capture all the cards.

Battle

Difficulty rating
1

Number of players
2

Cards
52. Aces can be high or low (to be agreed at the beginning of the game).

To win
Capture all 52 cards.

To deal
Deal out all the cards so that each player gets 26 cards. If playing more than one game, take it in turns to deal.

To play
Each player holds his or her stack of cards face down, then turns the top card over. The highest card of the two wins, no matter what suit it is. Whoever wins both cards, puts them at the bottom of his or her stack. If two cards of the same rank are drawn (that is, two Queens or two fours, and so on), then the cards are put on one side and are won by the winner of the next two cards.

The game is won by the first person to capture all the cards.

(Also see **War,** on page 336.)

Beggar Your Neighbour

Difficulty rating
1

Number of players
2

Cards
52

To win
Win all 52 cards.

To deal

Deal out all the cards so that each player gets 26 cards. If playing more than one game, take it in turns to deal.

To play

Each player puts his or her stack of cards face down on the table and takes it in turns to place a card, face up, in the middle. If one player turns up a Jack, Queen, King or an Ace, then the other player has to "pay" a certain number of cards on the pile, as follows:

Jack – one card
Queen – two cards
King – three cards
Ace – four cards

If all these cards are numerals (from two to ten), then the player winning them takes them and puts them at the bottom of his or her pile of cards and play continues as before. However, if one of the cards is another picture card or an Ace, then the tables are turned and the other player has to give up the required number of cards.

The game ends when one player has won all 52 cards.

Cheat (or I Doubt It)

Difficulty rating
2

Number of players
2-6

Cards
52 (Use two packs of cards for five or more players.)

To win
Be the first to run out of cards.

To deal
Deal out all the cards. It doesn't matter if some people have a few more cards than others. If playing more than one game, take it in turns to deal.

To play
The first player (this can be the youngest player, or the player to the immediate left of the dealer) starts by taking one, two, three or four cards out of his or her hand and placing them face down in the middle of the table, saying "One Ace", "Two Aces", "Three Aces" or "Four Aces" depending on how many cards he or she has put down. The next player then puts down from one to four twos and again states how many he or she is putting down. The third player then puts down from one to four threes, and so on. (Note: If two packs of cards are used, players can play up to eight cards at a time.)

The sequence of cards played can either run from Aces to Kings, or the sequence can start at any point and can run up or down the pack (so threes can be followed by twos or fours). Rules should be agreed at the beginning of the game.

If no one challenges what has been put down, the game continues. However, a player may challenge another player at any time by calling "Cheat!" or "I doubt it!". The cards that have just been played are then turned over to see whether the challenge is correct. If the player playing the cards has cheated, then that player must take all the cards in the pile and add them to his or her hand. If the player has not cheated, then the challenger must take the pile of cards. The play continues with the person who has won the challenge. A player *must* play when it is his or her turn, even if this means cheating! The game ends when a player successfully gets rid of all of his or her cards.

Variation of Cheat

In a variation of cheat, each person places just one card on the table at a time. The person who starts the game can name any card (such as "one four"). The next person must then follow with "one five", or "one four", and so on. A player may challenge another at any time. If the challenge is correct, the person who has cheated must take all the cards. If the challenge is not correct, the challenger takes them instead. The player winning the challenge starts the next sequence of cards, playing any card he or she likes. The player who gets rid of all of his or her cards first wins the game.

Go Fish

Difficulty rating
2

Number of players
3-6

Cards
52

To win
Form the most sets of cards of four of a kind (such as four Aces, four tens, or four Jacks, and so on).

To deal
Deal out five cards to each player. The rest of the pack should be placed face down in the middle of the table, forming the stock.

To play
The player to the immediate left of the dealer starts. He or she asks one of the other players, by name, for some of his cards, such as "Michael, give me your tens." The player can only ask for a card of a certain rank if he or she has at least one card of that rank in his or her own hand.

If the other player has one or more of the rank of cards asked for, he or she must hand the card or cards over and the player who success-fully asked for them gets another turn. If the other player does not have any of that rank of cards, he or she says "Go Fish" and the player who unsuccessfully asked for them must take the top card from the pile of stock. The player to his or her immediate left then gets a turn to ask any other player for cards.

If a player gets four cards of the same rank, then he or she should show all four cards and place them on the table. If a player runs out of cards then he or she draws the top card from the pile of stock and can ask another player for a card of the same rank. When there are no more cards in the stockpile, a player who runs out of cards is out of the game.

The game ends when, between them, the players have formed all 13 sets of cards. The player with the most sets wins.

Go Fish Variation

Go Fish can be simplified for very young players by forming pairs instead of sets of four.

The dealer deals out the whole pack of cards. It does not matter if they do not come out evenly. When it is a player's turn, he or she asks for one card by rank, saying, for example "Ella, give me a ten." If the player who has been asked for the card has it, then he or she must hand it over. When a player has a pair of cards, then he or she places it face down on the table in front of him or her.

The winner is the player with the most pairs at the end of the game.

Memory or Concentration

Difficulty rating
1

Number of players
2-6

Cards
52

To win
Gain the most pairs of cards.

To deal
Shuffle the cards and deal them, face down, all over the table, so that no two cards overlap.

To play
Each player takes it in turns to turn over two cards. If the two cards match in rank (for example, two Aces, or two tens), then the player wins the pair of cards and has another turn. If they do not match, the player turns them over so that they are again face down in the same position, and the next player has a turn.

The game ends when all the cards have been successfully matched into pairs, and the player with the most pairs of cards wins.

Variation of Memory
(sometimes called Pelmanism)

This is played the same way as Memory except that the player does not let the other player, or players, see the upturned cards. If they form a pair, the player shows them and keeps them. If they do not match, the cards are put face down in the same position and the next player has a turn. If a player wins a pair, he or she gets another turn.

My Ship Sails

Difficulty rating
1

Number of players
4–7

Cards
Seven cards for each player.

To win
Get seven cards of the same suit.

To deal

Deal out seven cards to each player. (The rest of the cards in the pack are not used.)

To play

Each player looks at his or her hand then, at the same time, each player passes one card face down to the player on his or her left and receives one card from the player on his or her right. The first player to get seven cards of the same suit wins the game by laying the cards face up on the table and calling "My Ship Sails."

Old Maid

Difficulty rating
I

Number of players
Two or more

Cards
51 (removing one of the four Queens)

To win
Avoid being left with a single, unpaired Queen (the Old Maid) at the end of the game.

To deal

Deal out all the cards. (It doesn't matter if one or more players have a few more cards.)

To play

Each player first matches up all the pairs in his or her hand and puts them in a pile on the table. If a player has three of a kind, he or she can only match two of them and must keep the third in his or her hand.

Once all the pairs have been discarded, the dealer fans out his or her cards and offers them, face down, to the player on his or her left. That player picks one of the offered cards. If the picked card makes a pair with one of the cards in the player's hand, then the pair is put down with the rest of the discarded pairs on the table. If not, it must stay in the player's hand and the player then offers it, with the rest, to the next player.

When a player's last card is taken, he or she drops out of the game. The game ends when one player is left with the odd Queen, or the Old Maid.

Pig

Difficulty rating
1

Number of players
3–13

Cards
Four of a kind for each player in the game

To win
Get four of a kind or be the first to notice when someone else has got four of a kind.

To deal
Shuffle the cards and deal them all out so that each player has four cards.

To play
Each player looks at his or her cards then, at the same time, passes one unwanted card face down to the player on his or her left and receives one card from the player on his or her right. The play continues like this until one player gets four cards of the same suit. That player then puts his or her finger on the tip of his or her nose. Once the other players have noticed this, they too stop passing cards and put their fingers to their noses. The player who is the last to notice and put a finger to his or her nose loses the game.

Sequence

Difficulty rating
l

Number of players
2–10 (4–5 is best)

Cards
52, with Aces high.

To win
Be the first to play all your cards.

To deal
Take it in turns to deal the cards. The dealer deals out all the cards. It does not matter if they do not come out evenly.

To play
Either the youngest player or the player to the immediate left of the dealer starts, playing his or her lowest card of any suit. The next player must play the next highest card in that suit, or miss a turn. Play continues around the table with each player either playing, if possible, or missing a go. The player completing a sequence with an Ace starts the next sequence, again playing his or her lowest card first.

The first person to play all of his or her cards shouts "Out" and wins the game.

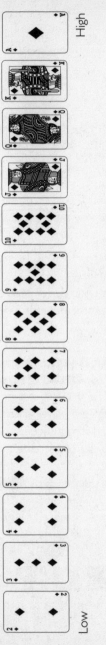

An example of a card sequence, with Aces high, and twos low.

Snap

Difficulty rating
1

Number of players
2-8

Cards
52

To win
Win all the cards.

To deal
Deal out all the cards. It doesn't matter if some players have a few more than others.

To play
Each player keeps his or her pile of cards face down on the table just in front of him, or can hold it in his hand. Taking it in turns, and playing as fast as possible, each player flips over his or her top card and drops it onto a common pile in the middle of the table. If a card that has just been played matches the card immediately below it (for example, an Ace on an Ace, or a ten on a ten), then the first person to call "Snap" wins the whole pile of cards and puts them at the bottom of his or her stack.

A player who runs out of cards is either out of the game or may be allowed to stay in the game to try to win the next "Snap" (rules to be agreed before the game begins).

If two or more players shout "Snap" at the same time, or if a player calls "Snap" by mistake, then the pile of cards in the middle of the table is put to one side as a "pool". Play continues as before but, in addition to matching cards in the central pile, if a card just played matches the top card of the pool, then a player can call "Snap pool" and win the pile of cards in the pool.

The game ends when one player wins all the cards.

Snap Variation

In a variation of Snap, each player takes it in turns to turn over their top card as fast as possible but, instead of putting it on a central pile in the middle of the table, he or she puts it on an individual pile just in front of him or her. If a card just played matches a card on any of the other player's piles of cards, then the player calling "Snap" wins the other player's pile of cards.

If someone calls "Snap" at the wrong time, then they should either pay a forfeit of one card to the player of the last card, or their upturned pile of cards can be put on one side as a "pool". The pool can be won by any player successfully spotting and calling "Snap pool".

A player who runs out of cards is either out of the game or may be allowed to stay in the game to try to win the next "Snap" (rules to be agreed before the game begins).

Snip, Snap, Snorem

Difficulty rating
I

Number of players
Any number, but 3–7 players is best

Cards
52

To win
Be the first to play all your cards.

To deal
The dealer (chosen by cutting the cards, with the person cutting the highest card dealing first) deals out all the cards one at a time. It doesn't matter if they do not come out evenly.

To play
The player to the immediate left of the dealer starts by playing any card. The next player must try to match that card by playing a card of the same rank. For example, if the first player plays a three, then the next player must play a three. If that player cannot play a three, then he or she says "Pass" and misses a turn.

The play continues around the table, with each person playing or passing. The first player to match the card in play calls "Snip", the next player to match the card calls "Snap", and the fourth (and final) player to match the card calls "Snorem" and starts the next round. A player can only play one card at a time, even if he or she holds two or more cards of the same value as the card in play.

The first player to play all his or her cards wins the game.

Variation of Snip, Snap, Snorem

In some games of Snip, Snap, Snorem, a player may play all his or her cards of the same value as the card in play at a time, calling out "Snip, Snap" or "Snap, Snorem" depending on whether they are playing the second and third or third and fourth cards of the sequence.

Stealing Bundles

Difficulty rating
1

Number of players
2 – 4

Cards
52

To win
Collect the most cards, or "bundles".

To deal
The dealer deals out four cards to each player, one at a time.

The dealer then places the next four cards from the pack face up in a row in the middle of the table. The rest of the pack is placed face down near the dealer.

To play

Each player looks at his or her cards and sorts them out by rank.

The player to the immediate left of the dealer starts. If the player has a card in his or her hand that matches one of the four cards in the middle of the table by rank (for example, a King and a King, or a two and a two), then he or she can take the card from the centre and place it and his or her own card face up on the table nearby to start a "bundle".

The next player then has a turn.

If two or three cards in the centre of the table are of the same rank, then a player holding another card of that rank can capture all the cards in the middle at the same time.

If a player holds a card that is the same rank as the top card in another player's bundle, then the player can capture the other player's whole bundle with that card.

If a player cannot capture a card from the centre or another player's bundle, then the player must "trail" a card by placing it face up in the middle of the table.

Players take it in turns to play, playing one card at a time. When a player "steals" a card or cards, he or she places them on his or her bundle, with the top card face up.

When each player has played his or her first four cards, the dealer deals out another four cards to each player, one at a time. However, no more cards are dealt to the centre of the table.

Play continues until all the cards have been dealt out and played. The player with the most cards in his or her bundle at the end of the game wins.

The Earl of Coventry

Difficulty rating
I

Number of players
any number, but 3–7 players is best.

Cards
52

To win
Be the first to play all your cards.

To deal
The dealer deals out all the cards, one at a time. It does not matter is some players have an extra card.

To play
All the players look at their cards and sort them out by rank.

Either the youngest player in the game or the player to the immediate left of the dealer starts by playing any card from his or her hand.

The next player must either play a card of the same rank, or miss a turn.

The play continues around the table, with each person playing or passing. The game is the same as "Snip, Snap, Snorem" except for the words spoken by each player as he or she plays a card.

Any children playing would say the following, making up a rhyme:

On playing the first card in a set of four (for example, a six):

"There's as good as six can be."

On playing the second card:
"There's a six as good as he."

On playing the third card:
"There's the best of all the three."

On playing the fourth and final card in the set:
"And there's the Earl of Coventry!"

Any adults playing can try to make up different rhymes as they play a card, such as:
"There's a six from the deep blue sea."
or
"There's the best of all to me."

If an adult does not manage to make up a rhyme that is accepted by the other players then he or she is not allowed to start a new round. Instead, the player sitting to his or her left gets a turn.

War

Difficulty rating
1

Number of players
2

Cards
52. Aces can be high or low (to be agreed at the beginning of the game).

To win
Capture all 52 cards.

To deal
Deal out all the cards so that each player gets 26 cards. If playing more than one game, take it in turns to deal.

To play
In this variation of War (see opposite), each player holds their stack of cards face down and, at the same time, turns their top card over. The highest card wins, no matter what suit it is, and the captured cards are put at the bottom of the winner's pile. If two cards are the same rank, then each player turns a second card face down and a third card face up. The player with the highest card then wins all six cards. If the cards turned up are again the same rank, then each player turns another card face down and another face up. The player with the highest card then wins all ten cards, and so on.

The war is won by the first person to capture all the cards.

War for Three

To play war with three players, remove any card from the pack and deal out three equal hands of 17 cards to each player. The game is played in the same way as War. If any two out of three cards turned up are the same rank, then all three players turn one card face down and one face up to win the cards in play. If all three cards turned up at a time are the same rank, then each of the three players turns *two* cards face down and one card face up. The highest card wins the rest.

In this game of War, both players first turn up tens, then threes. The player turning up the Jack wins all ten cards.

Children's Card Games II

(for older children)

Although many older children will easily be able to grasp the rules of basic Hearts, Whist, and Rummy and enjoy playing many of the games found in earlier sections of the book, the following games are traditionally viewed as children's games. Like those in the previous section, however, they're great fun for all members of the family – no matter what age.

Authors

Difficulty rating
2

Number of players
2–5

Cards
52

To win
Win the most sets of cards, called books. (A book is four cards of the same rank, such as four tens, or four Queens.)

To deal
The dealer shuffles the cards then deals them all out, face down on the table. It does not matter if each player does not have exactly the same number of cards.

To play
Before play, each player sorts out his or her cards, matching up cards of the same rank. If a player has four cards of the same rank, he or she can place the set, or "book" face down on the table. Before doing this, he or she should show the cards to the rest of the players.

Starting with either the youngest player or the player to the immediate left of the dealer, each player takes a turn to ask another player for a card, one at a time, by its rank and by its suit.

For example, a player might ask another player, "Nicola, give me the Queen of diamonds." If the player gets the card he or she has asked for then that player gets another turn. If the player does not get the card, then the player sitting to his or her immediate left gets a turn.

Once a player gets the fourth card in a book, he or she shows the other players all the cards in the set and places them face down on the table. Books should be placed slightly overlapping and sideways to each other so that they are easy to count at the end of the game.

The player with the most books win.

This game is also known as "Happy Families" and is similar to *"Go Fish"* on page 320 but requires more skill and a good memory!

Card Dominoes or 7s

Difficulty rating
I

Number of players
3–8

Cards
52. Kings rank high and Aces low

To win
Be the first to play all of your cards.

To deal
Deal out all the cards one at a time, face down, starting with the player on the dealer's left and moving clockwise around the table. If playing more than one game, take it in turns to deal.

To play
Players look at the cards in their hand and sort them out into suits

and sequences within each suit. The player who has been dealt the seven of diamonds starts the game by placing it face up in the centre of the table. The next player can then either place the eight or the six of diamonds on the seven, or can place another seven of any suit alongside. Each player takes it in turn to add a card to any sequence. Each sequence of cards ends with a King at the top and an Ace at the bottom. If a player cannot play any card, he or she misses a turn. However, if a player can play a card, then he or she must do so.

The first player who plays all his or her cards wins the game but the game continues until all four suit sequences have been completed.

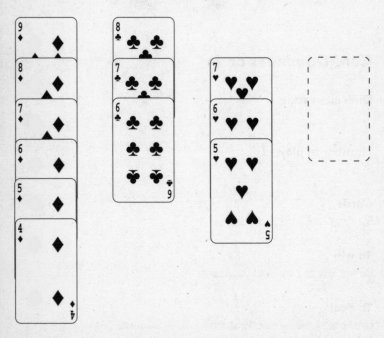

In this game of card dominoes, one player has not yet played the seven of spades because he or she does not hold high or low spades and hopes to make the other players miss a turn.

Chase the Ace

Difficulty rating
1

Number of players
3–10

Cards
52, with Kings ranking high and Aces low.

To win
Avoid holding the lowest card at the end of the game.

To deal
Deal out one card to each player in turn. Take it in turns to deal the cards.

To play
Each player takes it in turns to play, starting with the player sitting to the immediate left of the dealer. A player may either keep his or her card if it's a King or a card of a high rank or ask to exchange it with the card held by the player on his or her left. If the card held by the first player is a King then the player must turn it face up and can "Stand." The second player may only refuse to exchange his or her card with that of the player asking for it if the card is a King. If this is the case, then the King must be shown.

When it is the dealer's turn, he or she may either keep his or her card ("Stand"), or exchange it with another card taken from the top of the pack or cut from the middle of the pack (to be decided at the beginning of the game).

Each player then shows his or her cards and the player holding the lowest card loses a life. If more than one player holds the lowest cards in play, then each player loses a life.

Chase the Ace Variation

In some variations, if the dealer exchanges his or her card for another from the pack and gets a King, then the King counts lower than an Ace and only the dealer loses a life in that game.

Crazy Eights

Difficulty rating
1

Number of players
2–6

Cards
52, with Aces ranking low and counting as one point in a scoring game. Two packs of cards can be used if there are seven or more players.

To win
Be the first to get rid of your cards and score 500 points over the whole game.

To deal
The pack of cards is cut to determine the dealer, with the person cutting the highest card dealing first. The dealer deals out five cards to each player, one at a time. The remaining cards are stacked face down in the middle of the table and the top card of the stack is turned face up in a new pile alongside (the discard pile) to start the game.

To play
Each player takes it in turn to play, starting with the player to the immediate left of the dealer. Following the turned-up card, the player must either play a card of the same suit, a card of the same value, or an eight.

The eight is a "wild card" and can be played on any card at any time during the game. The person who plays it can then name the suit that must be played by the next player.

The first person to get rid of all his or her cards calls "Crazy Eights" and wins the hand. The first person to score an agreed number of points (usually 500) wins the game.

To score Crazy Eights
Points are scored by the person calling "Crazy Eights" by adding up the points value of the cards still held by the other players at the end of the hand.

Eight – 50 points each
King, Queen and Jack – 10 points each
Other cards, including Ace – face, or pip, value (ten points for a ten, nine for a nine, and so on, down to one point for an Ace).

(Also see **Go Boom!** on page 346 and **Switch** on page 366.)

Go Boom!

Difficulty rating
1

Number of players
2–6

Cards
52, with Aces ranking low and counting as one point in a scoring game.

To win
Be the first to get rid of your cards or score an agreed number of points

To deal
The pack of cards is cut to choose the dealer, with the person cutting the highest card dealing first. The dealer deals out the cards one at a time, according to the number of players:
8 cards each if there are three or four players
7 cards each if there are five players
6 cards each if there are six players
The remaining cards are stacked face down in the middle of the table.

To play
Each player takes it in turns to play, starting with player to the immediate left of the dealer. That player leads with the first card, placing it face up in the middle of the table. The other players must then play a card of either the same suit or the same rank. For example, if the first player leads with a Jack of diamonds, then the next player must put down any other diamond or another Jack. Tricks have no value and, once played, the played cards are put into a discard pile. The person who "wins" the last trick, by playing the highest card or matching the first card in rank plays the first card of the next trick.

If a player cannot play, then he or she must pick up the top card from the pile of stock and add it to his or her hand. A player must keep doing this every time it is his or her turn until he or she gets a card that can be played. If a player cannot play once the stock has been used up, then he or she misses a turn and says "Pass."

The first person to get rid of all his or her cards shouts "Boom!" and wins the game.

To score Go Boom
In some variations of Go Boom! points are scored by the first person going boom by adding up the points value of the cards still held by all the other players.

King, Queen and Jack – 10 points for each card
Other cards, including Ace – face, or pip, value (ten points for a ten, nine for a nine, and so on, down to one point for an Ace)

The first person to reach an agreed number of points (say 250) wins the game.

Knockout Whist

Difficulty rating
1

Number of players
2–7

Cards
52, with Aces ranking high.

To win

Stay in the game the longest.

To deal

Deal out seven cards to each player and turn over the next card to find out the trump suit.

To play

Each player takes it in turns to play, starting with the dealer. The dealer plays, or leads, with any card in his or her hand. The other players must then follow suit if they can. If they cannot follow suit, they can discard a card and lose the trick or play a trump card. The highest lead card or the highest trump, if a trump card is played, wins the trick.

If a player has not won any tricks at all, then he or she is knocked out of the game. The winner of the most tricks picks up all the cards, shuffles them, and deals out six cards to each player. The dealer then looks at his or her hand and chooses the new trump suit. Play continues as before, with any player who takes no tricks being knocked out of the game. The player winning the most tricks, deals the next hand, chooses trumps and plays the first card of the new hand.

The number of cards dealt to each player in the game decreases by one each time. The winner is the person still left in the game after all the other players have been knocked out.

Non-dealer's hand

Dealer's hand

Winning tricks

In this sample hand of Knockout Whist, two players have four cards each. The dealer chooses trumps – spades – and leads with the first card. The other player follows suit and loses the first trick. The dealer then plays his or her trump Ace to force the other player to play any trumps in his or her hand. The dealer then wins the remaining two tricks – and the game – because the other player cannot follow suit and better the cards.

Knockout Whist Variation

There are many different versions of Knockout Whist. In some games, the first player to be knocked out is given a "dog's chance". This mean he or she gets dealt one card in the next hand and can play it at any time to win a trick. If that player succeeds in winning a trick, then he or she is back in the game for the next hand.

(Also see **Crazy Eights** on page 344 and **Switch** on page 366.)

Liberty Fan-Tan

Difficulty rating
1

Number of players
3–8

Cards
52

To win
Be the first player to play all your cards.

To deal
The dealer deals out all the cards to each player, one at a time and face down.

To play

Each player looks at his or her cards and sorts them into suit and sequences within each suit.

The game is played in the same way as Card Dominoes (see page 341), except that the first player does not need to begin the game by playing a seven but can play any card and all the cards in one suit must be played before playing the first card of a new suit.

The next player must then play the next higher card in the sequence. For example, if the first card is the ten of diamonds, then the second player must play the Jack of diamonds if he or she holds it. If the second player has played the Jack, then the third player must play the Queen. To complete each sequence, Aces are played onto Kings, followed by twos, threes, and so on.

The player playing the thirteenth and final card of a sequence can play the first card of another suit. All the cards of that suit must then be played before starting the third, and so on.

Liberty Fan-Tan is often played with counters. If a player is unable to follow suit, then he or she must pay one counter into a pile in the centre of the table to form a "pool".

The winner is the first player to play all of his or her cards. That player then wins all the counters in the pool.

Linger Longer

Difficulty rating
I

Number of players
3–6 players (but best with 4 or 6)

Cards
52, with Aces high.

High   Low

Ranking of cards in Linger Longer

To win
Be the last player in the game holding any cards.

To deal
The dealer is chosen by cutting the cards, with the player cutting the highest card dealing first.

The dealer deals out the cards one at a time and face down to each player in turn, dealing out as many cards as there are players in the game. For example, if there are six players, then each player gets six cards.

The rest of the cards are placed face down in a pile on the table, to form the stock.

The dealer turns up his or her last card so that the other players can see it. The suit of the last card then becomes the trump suit for the hand. A trump card beats any card of any other suit.

To play

The player sitting to the immediate left of the dealer starts by playing one card face up in the middle of the table. Each of the other players then plays one card in turn. The set of cards is called a trick.

Each player must play a card of the same suit as the first card (called the lead card) if they can. If they cannot, they can play a trump card if they hold one. If a player cannot play a card of the same suit as the lead card and does not hold a trump card, then he or she plays any card.

The highest card of the suit of the lead card wins the trick unless a player plays a trump card, in which case the trump card wins the trick. If two players play trump cards, then the highest trump card wins the trick.

The player winning a trick, picks up all the cards in it and places them face down on the table in front of him or her.

He or she then takes the top card from the pile of stock and plays any card from his or her hand to start the next trick. The trump suit remains the same throughout the game.

A player who runs out of cards must drop out of the game. The last player to be holding any cards after all the other players have dropped out wins the game.

Lead card

Trick won by the Ace of
spades (the third and fifth
players do not hold any
spades or trump cards and
must discard)

Lead card

Trick won by the four of
hearts (the trump suit)

Examples of tricks in Linger Longer (five players)

Newmarket

Difficulty rating
I

Number of players
3–8

Cards
52, plus the Ace, King, Queen and Jack of different suits from another pack (usually the Ace of spades, King of clubs, Queen of hearts and the Jack of diamonds), which are placed face up in the centre of the table. Aces rank low.

To win
Get rid of all your cards and win chips, or counters, from the other players.

To deal
The dealer deals out all the cards one at a time to each player and deals an extra, dummy hand. It does not matter if the cards do not come out evenly (although in some versions, any extra cards are dealt to the dummy hand).

To play
Before the game starts, each player antes one chip, or counter, into the kitty and also places chips on one or more of the four "pay" cards. (In some versions, each player must place at least one counter on every card.)

The dealer looks at his or her hand and has the option of exchanging it for the dummy hand (he or she must make the decision to exchange it without looking at the dummy hand). If the dealer exchanges his or her hand, the rejected hand is put on one side and the game begins. If the dealer decides not to exchange his or her original hand, then the dummy hand (still unseen) can be bought by any of the other players for an agreed sum. (Price to be agreed at the beginning of the game.) The option to buy the hand passes around the table starting with the player to the immediate left of the dealer.

The player holding the lowest diamond starts the game by placing it face up on the table and stating its rank and suit (such as "two of diamonds). The holder of the next-highest diamond then plays it, again stating its rank and suit. If a player holds more than one card in the sequence, then he or she can play them all one after the other.

Play continues in this way, with players placing their cards in a pile in front of them, rather than in a common pile in the centre of the table, until no one can continue the sequence (because the next card is contained in the dummy hand). If no one can continue, then the player playing the last card can play a new card, starting with the lowest card held in a suit of the opposite colour. If the player does not hold any cards in the required colour, then the player to his or her immediate left gets a turn to play. If he or she does not hold an appropriate card, then the play passes to the left round the table.

A sequence also ends when a player plays one of the "pay" cards (an Ace, King, Queen or Jack that exactly matches one of the cards on the table). Once a player has played a "pay" card, then he or she wins all the counters staked on that card and starts a new sequence, again with the lowest card held of a different colour.

The first player to play his or her last card wins the kitty. If a sequence ends and none of the players hold a card of the opposite colour, then no one wins the kitty and it is carried forward to the next hand and increased.

Racing Demon

Difficulty rating
I

Number of players
2–6 players

Cards
52 cards for each player in the game (preferably with different pictures on the back of each pack)

To win
Be the first to use up your pile of 13 cards.

To deal
Each player shuffles his or her own deck and cards and deals 13 cards face down on the table. This pile of 13 cards is then turned face up and straightened so only the top card is showing. The player then deals four cards from the pack face up on the table in a row alongside.

To play
Playing as fast as possible, each player tries to use up his or her pile of 13 cards (the "demon" pile). Players do not take it in turns to play but simply play any cards they can as quickly as possible. Cards can be played as follows:

• Aces are played to the centre of the table. Cards are built up on each Ace in suits, so the two of diamonds can go on the Ace of diamonds, and the three on the two, and so on.
• Cards are played to the row of four face-up cards in descending order in alternate colours. For example, a red eight (either diamonds or hearts) can be played on the nine of spaces, then a black seven (spades or clubs) on the eight.

A player can play the top card of the demon pile to the centre of the table or onto one of the piles of four. Cards can be played from any of the piles of four (as long as they are the last cards in each sequence) to the centre of the table. If a player uses up all the cards in one of the four sequences, then he or she uses the top card in the demon pile to fill the gap. If a player cannot play, then he or she turns up cards from the stock, three at a time, and keeps doing this until he or she turns up cards that can be played.

Once the pile of stock has been used up, then it is turned over and dealt out again in sets of threes.

The first person to use up all the cards in his or her demon pile shouts "Out" and wins the game.

To score Racing Demon
There are different ways of scoring Racing Demon.
• Each player counts out how many cards he or she has played into the middle of the table, on the Aces, and how many cards are left. His or her score is the difference between these two numbers. The winner is the player with the highest score.
Or
• Points are awarded as follows:
– One point for every card played into the middle of the table on the Aces.
– Ten points for any King played into the middle of the table.
– Two points deducted for any card left in the demon pile.
The player with the highest score wins.

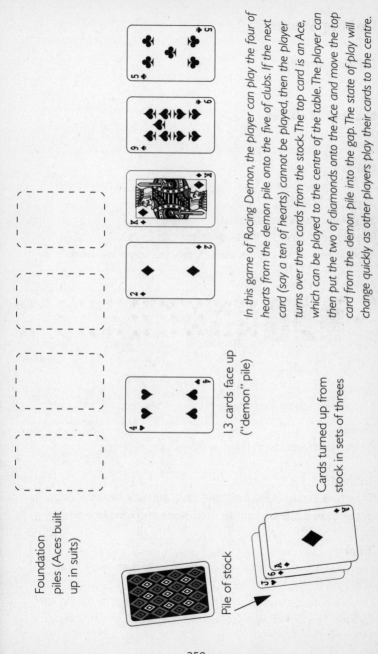

Foundation piles (Aces built up in suits)

13 cards face up ("demon" pile)

Cards turned up from stock in sets of threes

Pile of stock

In this game of Racing Demon, the player can play the four of hearts from the demon pile onto the five of clubs. If the next card (say a ten of hearts) cannot be played, then the player turns over three cards from the stock. The top card is an Ace, which can be played to the centre of the table. The player can then put the two of diamonds onto the Ace and move the top card from the demon pile into the gap. The state of play will change quickly as other players play their cards to the centre.

Rolling Stone

Difficulty rating
I

Number of players
4–6

Cards
52, but removing cards from the pack depending on the number of players, as follows:
Six players – take out the twos
Five players – take out the twos, threes and fours
Four players – take out the twos, threes, fours, fives and sixes

High   Low

Ranking of cards in Rolling Stone

To win
Be the first player to get rid of all your cards.

To deal
The player cutting the highest card from the pack deals the cards. He or she deals out eight cards to each player, singly and face down.

To play
Each player looks at his or her cards and sorts them out by suit.

The player to the immediate left of the dealer starts by playing any card from his or her hand face up into the middle of the table.

The next player must play a card of the same suit if possible. If all the players can follow suit, the group of cards on the table (called the trick) is piled face down on the table in a wastepile. The player playing the highest card in the trick then plays the first card of the next trick.

If a player cannot play a card of the same suit as the first, or lead, card, then that player must pick up all the cards played so far in the trick and add them to his or her hand. That player then plays the first card of the next trick using one of the cards already held in his or her hand (not one of the cards just picked up).

The first player to run out of cards wins the game.

Slapjack

Difficulty rating
1

Number of players
2–6

Cards
52

To win
Capture all the cards.

To deal
Each player takes it in turns to deal the cards. The dealer deals all the cards to each player in turn. It doesn't matter if they do not come out evenly.

To play

Each player puts his or her pile of cards face down on the table. Taking it in turns and playing as fast as possible, each player takes one card off his or her pile and puts it face up in a pile in the middle of the table. Whenever a Jack is played, the first person to slap his or her hand over it (Slapjack!) wins all the cards in the central pile. He or she then shuffles this pile with his or her own pile of cards and has the next turn.

If two people slap the Jack at the same time, the winner is the person with his or her hand underneath, on the Jack.

If a player slaps a card that isn't a Jack, then he or she must give one card off his pile to the player who played that card.

A player who has run out of cards is allowed one more chance to slap a Jack during the next round. If the player fails to slap a Jack, then he or she is out of the game.

The player winning all the cards or the player holding the most cards after an agreed time limit is the winner of the game.

Spit

Difficulty rating
1

Number of players
2

Cards
52

To win

Be the first player to run out of cards.

To deal

Players choose the first dealer by cutting the pack of cards, with the player cutting the highest card dealing first.

The dealer deals out all the cards, one at a time.

Each player then arranges his or her cards as follows:

Three cards are placed face down in a row from left to right, then the next card is placed face up.

Two cards are placed face down in another row slightly overlapping the first, then the next card is placed face up.

One card is placed face down, again slightly overlapping the first, then the next card is placed face up.

A final, single card is placed face up.

The remaining cards are then placed in a pile (the stockpile) to the left of each player.

To play

Once each player has laid out his or her cards, one player shouts "Spit!" and both players play cards from their layout onto either of the piles in the centre of the table as fast as possible.

Cards must be played in sequence either running up or running down. For example, a seven or a five can be placed on a six, and a three or an Ace can be placed on a two. Either a King or a two can be placed on an Ace.

In the layout on page 365, player 1 could play his or her Jack, Queen then King onto the ten in the middle of the table unless player 2 plays his or her nine on it first.

Once a player plays a face-up card and exposes a face-down card underneath, he or she can turn the lower card face up and play it onto one of the piles in the middle of the table if possible.

When both players cannot play another card into the centre, one of them shouts "Spit!"

Each player then simultaneously turns up the top card from his or her pile of the stock and puts it on the face-up pile he or she started. Play then continues in the same way until neither player can play a card and one of the players calls "Spit!" again. Both players then simultaneously turn up another card, and so on.

If a player's stockpile is used up and the player wants to call "Spit" then he or she turns the pile in the middle of the table face down, places it to the left of his or her cards and uses it as a stockpile. The player can then call "Spit" and the game continues.

As soon as a player has managed to play all the cards from his or her opening layout, then he or she shouts "Out" and wins that round of the game.

The player winning the round picks up his or her stockpile and makes a new layout with the cards in it as before.

The other player must pick up both piles of cards in the middle of the table as well as the cards in hbis or her stockpile and those left in his or her layout.

The first player to play all of his cards wins the game.

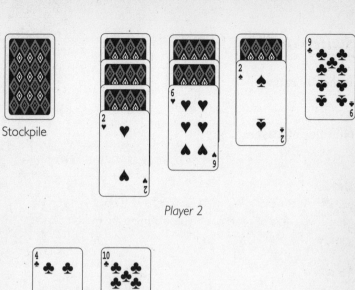

Player 2

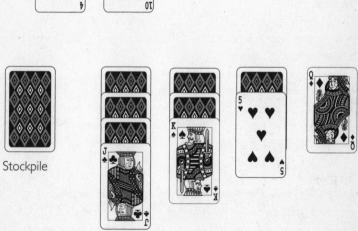

Player 1

In this opening layout of Spit, each player has laid out his or her cards and has placed the top card from his or her pile of stock into the middle of the table.

Switch or Black Jack

Difficulty rating
1

Number of players
2–6 players

Cards
52, with Aces ranking low and counting as one point in a scoring game. Two packs of cards can be used if there are more than six players.

To win
Be the first to play all your cards.

To deal
The dealer (chosen by cutting the cards, with the person cutting the highest card dealing first) deals out the cards one at a time according to the number of players:
12 cards each if there are two, three or four players
10 cards each if there are five or six players
The remaining cards are placed face down in a pile in the middle of the table and the top card is turned face up and placed next to the stockpile to start the game.

To play
The player to the immediate left of the dealer plays first, by playing one card from his or her hand on top of the upturned card. This card must be a card of the same rank or suit, or any Ace. Playing an Ace allows a player to change the suit, which need not be the same suit as the Ace just played.

In addition, playing certain cards has other rules, as follows:

• If a player plays a two, then the next player must also play a two. If unable to do so, the player must take two extra cards from the pile of stock and miss a turn. If the player can play a two, however, the following player must play another two or draw four cards from the stockpile. If all four twos are played one after the other, then the player whose turn is next must draw eight cards from the pile of stock.

• If a player plays a four, then the next player must either play a four or take four extra cards from the pile of stock and miss a turn. If another four is played, then the next player must take eight cards, and so on. If four fours are played one after the other, then the next player must draw sixteen cards from the pile of stock.

• If a player plays a Jack, this switches the direction of play from clockwise to anticlockwise (or back again if another Jack is played).

A player cannot play a Jack on a two or a two on a four to avoid changing the direction of play or picking up the required number of cards.

When a player plays his or her second-to-last card, he or she must immediately say "One left" or miss his or her next turn and take a card from the pile of stock instead. The first player to play all his or her cards wins the game.

To score Switch
The winner of each hand can score points by adding up the points value of the cards left in the other players' hands, as follows:
Ace – 20 points
Two, four or Jack – 15 points
King or Queen – 10 points
Other cards – face, or pip, value (ten points for a ten, nine for a nine, and so on)

The first person to reach an agreed total of points (say 500) wins the game.

Black Jack Variation

There are many variations of Black Jack, with different cards having different rules. The important things is to agree the rules before you begin the game.

For example, in some versions if a player plays a black Jack, the other player must pick up seven cards unless he or she has either
• another black Jack, which means the next player picks up fourteen cards.
• a red Jack, which nullifies the black Jack just played and means the player doesn't have to pick up any cards at all.

If the black Jack is used in this way, then another card – such as the King – becomes the "switch" card.

Another rule is that if a player plays a seven or an eight, then he or she gets another turn.

Index to the best number
of players for different games

Games for One

Good games for Two

Good games for Three

Good games for Four (played solo)

Good games for Four (played in partnerships)

Good games for Five

Good games for Three to Six or more (played in a round)

General index of card games

Index